Stags and Hens

omedy

Russell

To b

Samuel French – London
New York – Sydney – Toronto – Hollywood

ISBN 0 573 01609 7

Please see page vi for further copyright information.

STAGS AND HENS

First produced at the Everyman Theatre, Liverpool, in
October, 1978, with the following cast:

Linda	Anne-Louise Wakefield
Maureen	Barbara Peirson
Bernadette	Cecily Hobbs
Carol	Donna Champion
Frances	Lola Young
Dave	
Robbie	Philip Donaghy
Billy	Christopher Martin
Kav	Chris Darwin
Eddy	Edward Clayton
Peter	Richard Clay Jones
Roadie	

The play directed by **Chris Bond**
Designed by **Billy Meall**

The action of the play takes place in the Ladies' and
Gents' toilets in a Liverpool dance hall

ACT I Evening
ACT II Immediately after

Time—the present

AUTHOR'S NOTE

Although the use of music is not specified in the text, I envisage that in production, as the main doors are opened and closed, we would hear snatches of the music being played in the dance hall.

References to media people–eg Rod Stewart, Mick Jagger etc. can be updated.

W.R.

Stags and Hens was produced in London at the Young Vic in July 1984, with the following cast:

Maureen	Eithne Browne
Bernadette	Noreen Kershaw
Carol	Gilly Coman
Frances	Kate Fitzgerald
Linda	Anne Miles
Robbie	Nick Maloney
Kav	Graham Fellows
Billy	Ray Kingsley
Eddy	Matthew Marsh
Peter	Peter Christian
Roadie	Andrew Secombe
Dave	Vivian Munn

Directed by **David Thacker**
Décor by **Shelagh Killeen**

ACT I

The Ladies and Gents in a Liverpool dance hall. Evening

In the Gents, there are three full-length, bow-shaped urinals and one WC with a door, a mirror, a washbasin, a paper-towel dispenser, a metal basket for paper towels. In the Ladies, there are three WCs, a washbasin, make-up ledge, chairs, a long mirror, a paper-towel dispenser and basket. Windows are optional in the Ladies, but in the Gents there should be one fairly large reinforced window, and another small window in the WC. There is a corridor between the Ladies and Gents, with double doors which lead to the foyer. Upstage of these doors, the corridor leads backstage to the bandroom etc.

As the House Lights go down, Stevie Wonder's "Superstition" is playing. The song fades and we hear, coming in over it, the sound of girls singing

Girls (*off*) She's gettin' married in the morning
Ding dong the bells are gonna chime
Pull out his chopper
Oogh what a whopper
Get me to the church on time . . .

The girls come through the double doors and into the Ladies. Linda, the obvious subject of their song, goes straight into a WC and closes the door. The remaining girls begin to make-up

Maureen (*crying*) Congratulations Linda. Congratulations.
Bernadette What's up with you now?
Maureen I don't know.
Bernadette Cryin'! On a hen night! It's supposed to be a happy night.
Maureen (*bawling*) I am happy. I'm very happy . . . for Linda.
Carol (*calling out to Linda*) We're all happy for y'Linda. Ogh Lind, you lucky sod!
Frances Just imagine Lind, after tomorrow you'll have your own flat, your own feller. You'll be a married woman.
Bernadette You'll have your own front room, your own Hoover, your own telly.
Maureen (*crying*) Your own husband . . .
Carol Agh yeh. He's great Dave isn't he? He's a great feller. He's really dynamic isn't he?
Frances He's good lookin'.

Bernadette An' he's a worker isn't he? I mean he's not like some of them is he?

Carol They wouldn't lift a finger some of them, would they?

Bernadette Her feller's not like that though, is he?

Carol I'll bet he helps in the house an' that. I'll bet y'he does.

Bernadette Some fellers wouldn't would they? My feller doesn't. Wouldn't lift a bloody finger. He wouldn't get out that chair if the roof was comin' through. Idle, y'know, that type! The kids call him the reluctant plumber . . . never does a tap!

Frances Her Dave won't be like that though.

Carol Agh no, Dave'll be great in the house.

Maureen I'll bet he even helps when the little ones come along. (*She cries*)

Frances Will you shut it!

Bernadette For Christ's sake Maureen, tonight's supposed to be a celebration, not a wake.

Maureen I am celebrating. I'm celebrating for Linda. It's just . . . just that I wish it was me . . .

Frances Well never mind Maureen . . . your turn'll come.

Maureen (*brightening*) D'y'think so? D'y'really think so?

Frances Yeh . . . you'll be all right. You've just got to meet the feller who appreciates your sort of looks.

Maureen What sort of looks?

Frances Well y'know sort of er, y'know . . . (*looking round for assistance*) . . . er . . .

Carol (*calling*) Agh God . . . I'm so happy for y'Lind.

Bernadette I can't wait t'see her in church tomorrow.

Carol Agh I'll bet she looks lovely in white as well. Have y' seen her dress Mo?

Maureen When I was round there last week her mum said she'd show it me. But I couldn't bring meself to look. I would have cried. I cry very easily.

Frances We wouldn't have known.

Carol I saw it. Oh it's gorgeous, y'know, just off the shoulder.

Frances It's the new length isn't it?

Carol Y'know, with the lace, across here Mo.

Frances The back's lovely isn't it Carol?

Carol Oh the back's superb. It's got no back. Haven't you seen it Berni?

Bernadette No . . . I like to save it for the actual day. I like to get me first glimpse of it in Church.

Carol Agh that's nice isn't it eh? That's really nice Bern.

Bernadette (*calling*) We're all so happy for y'Linda.

Frances What makes it really special is that it's Linda.

Carol Ogh I know. I always thought Linda'd be the last one to get married, if she ever got married at all. Oh not 'cos she isn't eligible. She is, she's very eligible.

Bernadette She could have been a model if she'd wanted to.

Carol Ogh I know. No I'm not saying that. What I mean is . . . Linda was always like sort of independent wasn't she? Y'know what I mean?

Murmurs of agreement

Like she wouldn't take things seriously would she? An' then she just
announces that she's gettin' married. An' she's not in the club or anythin'
like that, is she?

Bernadette Love, Carol. Love changes you. Love makes you grow up.

Carol Tch. Ah ... I'm glad. I'm so glad for y'Linda.

Bernadette I know she'll be very happy with Dave. Now it'd be a different
matter if it was someone like my feller she was marryin'! Man? My feller?
He's an apology! I said to him, last night, I was feelin' a bit turned on,
y'know, an' he's lyin' there, snorin' again; that type he is, y'know, head
hits the pillow an' he's straight asleep. I looked at him, lyin' there an' I
said to him, I said ... "Hey, it's a bloody good job they didn't have the
Trades Descriptions Act when they christened you Dick!"

The girls laugh

Frances Go away Berni. The poor feller's probably worn out with you.
You'd be moanin' about not gettin' enough if y'were married to Rod
Stewart.

Bernadette You what? 'Ey I bet me an' Rod'd get on like a house on fire.

Carol Oh imagine bein' married to someone like Rod Stewart. You'd have
your own big house, servants, a swimming pool, all the clothes y'wanted.

Maureen It might all look glamorous Carol, but fame has its drawbacks
though.

Bernadette Eh, I'd risk it. Wouldn't you Carol ... whoa, spit on me Rod!

Maureen No, but honestly Berni, it's true y'know ... the price of fame is a
big one.

The girls shriek

What? ... What's up? Oh 'ey ... y'know I didn't mean it like that ...
that's awful ... eh ... look, I've smudged me eye now ... I've got half an
eye on me nose ...

Frances Oh come here. (*She does her make-up for her*)

Carol 'Ey ... what y'drinkin' tonight?

Maureen I'm goin' on brandy an' Babychams. I could drink them all night.

Frances Yeh, an'y' probably will knowin' you.

Carol You wanna try Pernod an' black, Mo. It's great.

Frances Y'don't wanna drink too much tonight. Save y'selves for tomorrow.

Carol The fellers won't be doin' that will they?

Bernadette Y'can bet they'll be pourin' it down them like it's goin' out of
fashion.

Maureen Where are they havin' the stag night?

Frances Dave wouldn't tell Linda where they were goin'.

Carol I'll bet they've gone to a stag club, watchin' those films ...

Bernadette Tch. An' here's us come to a borin' dance.

Carol Go way Berni. We don't wanna be watchin' blue films.

Bernadette 'Ey, you speak for yourself.

Maureen What are they like Carol?

Carol Horrible. All sex.

Bernadette Great!

Carol They're not like "Emmanuelle" Mo, that's a lovely film. But with the blue films it's just sex, y'know for the sake of it. With "Emmanuelle" it's like beautiful an' romantic, all in slow motion, now that's how sex should be. All soft an' in colour.

Bernadette That's how it should be Carol, but it never is love.

Carol It can be. With the right man it can. I'm not interested in fellers who want to make sex. I want a feller who makes love, not a feller who makes sex.

Maureen I just want a feller.

Bernadette Y'know when my feller was young——

Frances Young? Christ Berni he's only about thirty-two now, isn't he?

Bernadette Yeah, but I'm talkin' about young inside; I mean he might be young on the outside, but he's a geriatric inside. No, when me an' him were first married we went on a holiday to Devon. We went the pictures one night and saw this film where this couple kept goin' down to the shore and making love——

Maureen Ogh ... I seen that ... it's great—all the little waves are lappin' over them aren't they, an' the sun's settin', an' all the music an' that ... It's a great film that ...

Bernadette Really beautiful. Magic. So when it was over we come out the pictures an' me an' my feller walked down to the beach, an' honest to God it was just like the film, y'know, deserted it was, the beach. An' the sun was sinkin' into the horizon. There was nothin' but us an' the sound of the sea, just softly lappin' the beach.

Carol Agh isn't that lovely. It sounds like paradise.

Bernadette That's what it was like ... honest. That's just how I felt, like I was standin' on the edge of Paradise. (*She pauses*) An' my feller's got his arm around me, an' he sort of squeezed me an' he said, I'll always remember it, y'know what he said?

All the girls are wide-eyed in anticipation, shaking their heads

"Well are y'gettin' them off or what?"

The girls laugh

Frances 'Ey ... it'd be great on the films that wouldn't it? Imagine Ryan O'Neal to Ali McGraw? "Ey girl, d'y' fancy a legover?"

Laughter from the girls

Bernadette Y'see Carol, it's only half of it y'see in the films. I'll tell y'another thing the film didn't mention: the bloody sand gets everywhere!

Maureen (*laughing with the rest of them*) Agh we're having a great time aren't we? Aren't we eh?

Bernadette We were gonna stay down there in Devon. We didn't though. But y'wanna hear my feller. He's always goin' on about movin' down there—y'know if we go out together an' he has a few jars y'can't shut him up about Devon. I say to him, "Well let's do it, come on, let's go" ... but he wakes up the next day and pretends he never said it. I suppose we'll live and die round here.

Carol It's a dump isn't it eh? It's like this place—Christ look at it. Why didn't we go to a club?

Frances Linda wanted to come here. It's her hen night, she chooses where we go.

Carol Why did she choose here though? God it's dyin' on its feet this place.

Frances There's a group on after the disco though, isn't there? She said she wanted to dance to live music not just to records.

Carol I hate groups, they're not half as good as the records. What have they got a group on for?

Frances They tryin' t'bring some life back t'the place.

Bernadette It used to be all groups here y'know. Y'couldn't get in this place at one time. It was alive.

Carol Y'couldn't tell that now could you?

Bernadette It's dyin' this place is.

Frances It's dead.

Carol They'd have to do more than just stick a group on after the disco if they wanted this place to come alive again.

Bernadette It's like everythin' else round here Carol, the life's just drainin' away from the place, but no-one ever does anythin' about it. It's like round our way, y'know what they do if a wall's fallin' down—they give it a coat of paint. They do.

Carol Well I think we should've gone to a club.

Frances Well we can do that afterwards. But Linda wanted to come here first.

Maureen 'Ey ... wouldn't it be awful if the fellers turned up as well?

Carol (*shocked*) Oh God Maureen don't say things like that. If Linda saw Dave on her weddin' night, that'd be it, y'know.

Maureen I know ... that's what I'm sayin'—y'marriage would be doomed to perpetual bad luck if y'saw your feller the night before.

Bernadette 'Ey ... maybe that's what happened to me eh?

Frances What's she doin' in there anyway? (*She bangs on the WC door*) Linda ...

No answer

Linda! Linda are you comin' out of there?

Linda No!

As they sit waiting for Linda the Lights cross-fade to the Gents. We see the foyer doors swing open. Robbie, Billy and Kav are struggling to get the legless Dave into the Gents

Robbie (*to Billy*) Hold the door. Just hold the door will y'.

He does so

Kav Jesus!

They get him through the swing doors which Billy continues to hold open

Billy No ... y'see the problem is that y'not manœuvring him right. You've got to manœuvre correctly. Yeh.

Kav I'll manœuvre you in a minute.

Billy What?
Dick What y'doin'?
Billy I'm holdin' the door like y'said. Yeh.
Robbie We're in now, dickhead! Come here will y'? Get hold.

He lets Billy take his place. He looks down at the stain on his trousers, holds open the door to the Gents. They begin to get him in

Agh look at that. Jesus! Curried bleedin' chicken all over me.
Kav It's disaster for you Robbie. Disaster.

Robbie begins to help get Dave into the Gents

An' that little one was givin' you the big eye on the way in.
Billy It's all physics y'see. I read about it. Yeh.
Robbie Was she? Which one?
Kav Know that little one in the cloakroom?
Robbie That little one? Looks like Bianca Jagger?
Kav Yeh . . . that's the one.
Robbie Was she givin' me the eye?

They try to get Dave into the WC

Billy (*as they do so*) No, see . . . he's a dead weight . . . you've got to take that into account. Yeh.
Robbie I thought she was givin' me the eye, that one.
Kav Y'can forget now though can't y'? You've got no chance with spewed curry all over y'. Y'll stink all night like a Chinese chippy.
Robbie All right, all right. I'll wash it off. Come on, get him sorted out, then I can get me kecks clean.

They get him into the WC

Where's Eddy? He should be here givin' us a hand.
Kav He went the bar.
Robbie As long as he's not tryin' to chat up that little Bianca one.
Kav No way, I know what Eddy's like. He never chats tarts.
Billy He gets one when he wants one though. Yeh.
Kav Yeh, but he doesn't chat them up. He just waits till the end of the night, sees one an' says "Come here you!" An' they do y'know. But he won't waste his time chattin' them up.
Robbie He'd have no chance anyway. Not with competition from me. See me when I get out on that floor. They can't take their eyes off me.
Kav They will when they smell that spewed curry all over y'.
Robbie (*to Billy*) That's you that soft lad! Gettin' us to go the Chinese before we start drinkin' instead of afterwards.
Billy No y' wrong there Robbie. Yeh. See, I said we should go to the Chinese first 'cos it puts a linin' on y'stomach.
Robbie Yeh. An' it's put a linin' all over my suit as well!
Kav Come on . . . lift him so his head's over the bowl.
Billy (*as they struggle with Dave*) I didn't know Robbie. I didn't know he'd start drinkin' Black Velvets. An' he'd been on double Southern Comforts

before that y'know. I said to him "That's a lethal combination that Dave". Yeh.

Robbie Come on . . . lift him . . . an' keep him over that side. If he gets me other leg I'm done for!

They manage to get him arranged. We see only his legs sticking out. They stand back

Billy You wanna put your fingers down your throat Dave.

Robbie You wanna stick y'fingers down your throat. An' keep them there. Give us all a rest.

Billy I'm only tellin' him Robbie. 'Cos if he got it all up he could start drinkin' again. He's not gonna have much of a stag night if he spends it all in here, is he?

Kav (*looking at Dave*) 'Ey it's a good job his tart can't see him now isn't it?

Robbie She'd just laugh, her, she's mental.

Kav She's a good laugh though isn't she? She's all right Linda is.

Robbie She drinks as much as him y'know. I was goin' out with this crackin' tart once, y'know, nice, smart girl she was. We went out on a foursome with Dave an' his tart. I got the first round in, asked them what they were havin'. This girl I'm with she said er, a Babycham or a Pony or somethin', y'know, a proper tarts' drink. Know what Dave's tart asked for eh? A pint of bitter! That's dead true that, she wasn't jokin'. I was dead embarrassed. I'm out with this nice girl for the first time an' Dave's tart's actin' like a docker.

Kav She is a laugh though isn't she?

Robbie Laugh. The one I was with, she never came out with me again after that. I said to Dave after, fancy lettin' your tart behave like that. "She's always the same," he said. "But she'll settle down when she's married." I wouldn't take the chance.

Billy They do calm down Robbie. Women, y'can't get a laugh out of them once they've turned thirty.

Kav (*beginning to draw on the wall*) I like Linda.

Robbie (*wetting paper towels and beginning to try a repair job on his trousers*) What y'doin' Kav?

Kav Just me name. (*He is beginning an elaborate scroll which is intended to form his name*)

Billy (*watching*) 'Ey that's dead good that. Yeh. I didn't know you could do that Kav. It's good that isn't it? (*He watches for a moment*)

Kav suddenly crosses it all out

Kav Agh . . .

Robbie He's a good artist Kav is.

Billy 'Ey don't cross it out. It's dead good that. Yeh.

Kav It was crap.

Billy I thought it was cracker.

Kav Useless. Y'shoulda seen the stuff I did in the Top Rank Suite. What was it like Robbie?

Robbie Didn't y'see that Billy? It was smart that was. Y'know he did a big drawin', didn't y' Kav, on the back of a bog door, covered the whole door it was . . .

Kav Took me weeks to do that y'know. Every time we went the Top Rank I spent longer in the bogs than I did on the dance floor.

Robbie It was like abstract wasn't it? Not like that stupid abstract stuff though—y'could see picture in it couldn't y'Kav?

Kav Even Eddy said that was good, didn't he? But then we went in there one week an' they'd had the painters in to paint out all the writin' in the bogs. They stippled all over me picture with Artex an' put up a sign sayin' they'd prosecute anyone found defacin' the place.

Billy How d'y'draw like that eh?

Kav I dunno. It's dead easy. I just do it.

Billy I wish I could draw like that . . . don't you Robbie.

Robbie Too right. I'd spend all day drawin' me own porny pictures.

Billy Ogh I can do them . . . gis y'pencil Kav. Yeh. (*He takes the pencil and begins drawing on the wall*)

Robbie (*inspecting his trousers*) Ah . . . look at that. It's gonna take ages to dry now.

Billy There's no rush anyway. We can't just leave Dave here can we?

Robbie On y'bike. He'll be all right. We can keep nippin' in to have a look at him. Where's Eddy anyway? He should be here. Dave's his best mate.

Kav Eddy doesn't like it when y'get pissed. It gets him narked.

Billy Eddy never gets legless himself though does he? It's 'cos he's captain of the team. He thinks he should set an example.

Kav He's dead professional Eddy, isn't he? An' he's dead serious about his football. He's dead serious about everything'.

Robbie It's only Sunday League though isn't it? I mean it's not professional football is it?

Kav Don't let Eddy hear y'say that.

Robbie (*showing his trousers to Kav*) That look all right or what?

Kav (*non-committal*) It's all right.

Billy Y'll never get that off properly with water Robbie. Y'need petrol. Yeh.

Robbie Well I'll tell y'what . . . why don't you sod off down the garage an' get a can!

Billy What? No, listen. If there were still petrol lighters you'd be OK wouldn't y'? It's all gas though now isn't it? See that's an example of where technology makes significant advances an' losses at the same time.

Robbie Yeh that's just what I was thinkin'.

Billy No listen, I read about it. See if they still had petrol lighters you'd be able to take the cotton wool out an' clean your kecks with it wouldn't y'? Yeh. You wouldn't be stinkin' of curry then.

Robbie Yeh. I'd just be stinkin' of friggin' petrol wouldn't I?

Billy No. It'd evaporate. Yeh.

Robbie I wish you'd bleedin' evaporate! (*He notices Billy's drawing*) What the fuck's that?

Billy It's a tart. With nothin' on! Yeh.

Kav She's got no arms or legs!

Billy I know.

Robbie An' where's her head?
Billy I don't do heads. I only do the important bits. I'm a primitive!
Robbie You're a fuckin' idiot. Y've given her three tits!
Billy Where?
Robbie (*pointing*) Where!
Billy That's her stomach.
Kav Well why's it got a nipple on it?
Billy That's not a nipple—it's a belly button.
Robbie Anyway soft lad, who told y'heads weren't important? The way a
tart looks, her face an' that . . . it's dead important. There's nothin' better
than a beautiful girl.
Billy They're all the same when y'get down to it though aren't they?
Robbie Get lost. When y'get married y'spend longer looking at them than
y'do screwin' them, don't y'? I'll tell y'la, when I get married she'll be a
cracker my missis will, beautiful.
Kav She might be a cracker when y'get married to her Robbie but she won't
stay that way.
Robbie She bleedin' will!
Kav Go 'way Robbie. Y'know what the tarts round here are like; before
they get married they look great some of them. But once they've got
y'they start lettin' themselves go. After two years an' a couple of kids,
what happens eh? They start leavin' the make-up off don't they, an'
puttin' on weight. Before y'know where y' are the cracker y' married's
turned into a monster.

Eddy enters through the double doors and heads for the Gents

Robbie My missis isn't gonna be like that. If any tart of mine starts actin'
slummy she'll be booted out on her arse. A woman has got a responsibi-
lity to her feller. No tart of mine's gonna turn fat.
Billy I like a bit of weight. Somethin' t'get hold of.

Eddy enters. He goes straight to the urinal

Kav What's the talent like out there Eddy?
Eddy I don't know about the talent. The ale's last!
Billy Yeh, y'know why that is Eddy? Eh? It's 'cos it's pumped up with top
pressure.
Eddy Is that right?
Billy Yeh. I'm a real ale man I am.
Eddy Who's smart idea was it to come here? We coulda stayed in the pub.
Robbie There's no talent in the pub Eddy.
Billy CAMRA. Y'know, the Campaign for Real Ale. I support that. I've
got a badge.
Robbie (*giving up the cleaning attempt*) What am I gonna do? That little
Bianca one's gonna be all over me in half an hour. What's she gonna say if
she can smell curry everywhere?
Kav Tell her it's the latest aftershave.
Eddy "Madras: For Men".
Robbie 'Ey yeh . . . "Things happen to a feller who uses Madras for Men."

Kav Yeh. Instead of gettin' y'oats y'get chicken byriani.
Robbie No danger. I'm on I am. See her givin' me the eye did y'?
Kav Yeh . . . it was me who told y'!
Eddy Tarts! Women!
Billy (*laughing*) He's always on about tarts him, isn't he Eddy?
Eddy Y'know your problem Robbie . . . y'were born with y' brains between y'legs.

Kav and Billy laugh

Robbie That's not a problem.
Eddy Isn't it?
Robbie What's wrong with likin' the women eh Eddy?
Eddy (*looking in at Dave*) Look at him! You'll end up like him Robbie. See him, he's the best inside player I've ever seen. But it's all over for him. Well, it will be after tomorrow.
Robbie Christ Eddy, he's gettin' married, not havin' his legs sawn off.
Eddy You just watch him over the next few months. I've seen it before. Once they get married the edge goes. Before long they start missing one odd game, not turnin' up. You mark my words. The next thing is they stop playin' altogether. They have t' take the kids out on a Sunday, or they go down the club at dinnertime, drinkin'. Or they just can't get out of bed 'cos they've been on the nest all night. Nah . . . it's the beginnin' of the end for him.
Billy (*approaching Eddy*) I'm not gonna get married Eddy I'm stayin' at home with me mam.
Kav Don't you think that woman's suffered enough?
Billy I'll still be there, playin' in defence, when I'm forty Eddy. Yeh. I keep meself fit I do.
Eddy I know y' do Billy. Y' not like Robbie are y'? Robbie's a tarts' man. You'll end up like Dave you will, Robbie.
Robbie Ah give it a rest will y' Eddy. Sunday League football isn't the be all and end all is it? This is supposed to be a stag night, not a pre-match pep talk.
Eddy Who the fuck are you talkin' to? I'll remember that Robbie, I'll remember that when I'm pickin' this week's team.
Billy (*after a pause*) Are y' droppin' him Eddy?
Kav Are y' Eddy?
Robbie I don't care!
Eddy Don't y'? Not even when there's an American Scout gonna be watchin' us?
Kav Watchin' our game Eddy? On Sunday?
Billy I'm at the top of me form y'know Eddy. Yeh.
Kav An American Scout Eddy?
Eddy There's talent scouts from America combin' this country lookin' for potential.
Kav 'Ey . . . we'll be without Dave. Dave won't be playin' on Sunday, will he?

Eddy That's his hard luck isn't it? If he wants t' be in Spain when we've got a scout watchin' us, that's his hard luck!

Robbie Ah come on Eddy . . . let's get out there . . . listen to a few sounds, it's great when the music's playin'. Come on, have a few jars an' a laugh an' that.

Eddy snorts and turns away

Look Eddy, I'm set up already with a smart little one, just like Bianca Jagger, isn't she Kav? She's bound to have a crackin' mate with her, Eddy. I'll have the little Bianca one, you take her mate.

Eddy What? Spend all night chattin' up some dumb tart, two hours of sufferin' her talkin' an' drinkin' an' dancin', just to get a poke at her. Sod off.

Billy (*at Robbie's shoulder*) I'll take her mate for y' Robbie.

Robbie On y' bike! You're a bleedin' liability you are.

Billy Well. You always go after the smartest tarts in the place. I get nervous with that type.

Robbie I've told y' haven't I? Always go for the crackers. Loads of fellers make that mistake, they see really smart tarts an' they think they've got no chance. But it's the opposite. If a tart looks really good, an' y' can see she's spent hours gettin' herself to look somethin' special it's 'cos she wants someone to tap off with her.

Billy But I just get shy Robbie.

Kav (*to Billy*) Come on. Me an' you it is. But listen . . . no standin' at the side of the floor all night. When I say go in, we go in . . . right?

Billy All right.

Robbie Come on.

The three of them move towards the door

Eddy 'Ey.

They stop

Hold on!

Pause

Where youse goin'?

Robbie What Eddy?

Eddy What about him? (*He indicates Dave*)

Robbie What about him?

Eddy (*after a pause*) Just gonna leave him here are y'?

The three of them, on the spot, look at each other

He's our mate isn't he?

Kav Course he is Eddy.

Robbie Yeh.

Eddy An' y' just gonna leave him here are y'? Y' gonna leave him like this while y' go off listenin' to cheap music an' chasin' tarts?

Robbie Ah 'ey Eddy . . .
Eddy Ah 'ey what? Y' just gonna fuck off on y' mate when he's incapable,
needs lookin' after.

Pause, Eddy looks at them

Kav He'll be all right Eddy.
Eddy That's loyalty for y' isn't it?

Pause

Robbie Well you look after him Eddy! We've had our turn. Christ we got
him in here didn't we? Look, spewed curry all over me best suit.
Eddy Haven't you heard of loyalty?

Pause. They can't move

Go on then . . . piss off. I'll look after him. I'm stayin' in the bar. I'll keep
nippin' in to see that he's all right.

Pause

Go on . . . sod off!

They don't move

It's last out there anyway. All it is is music, fuckin' music.
Billy I like music Eddy.
Eddy You would wouldn't y'. 'Cos y' fuckin' soft, like them! Go on then,
get out there, an' listen to it.

Pause

Kav What's wrong with music Eddy?
Eddy (*after a pause, looking at them*) Y'know what music does don't y'?
Robbie It makes y' feel good Eddy.
Eddy Makes y' feel good! Makes y' go soft.

Pause. Eddy looks at them

Robbie Come on Eddy, come with us. Dave'll be all right.
Kav There's a live group on after, Eddy.
Eddy (*turning to look into the WC*) Is there? I'll bet they're shite as well!
Robbie They're not a local band Eddy. They're up from London. They'll be
good.
Eddy They didn't look like Londoners to me. I just saw them comin' in.
They looked local. I thought I recognized one of them.
Robbie Nah . . . That'll be from off the telly Eddy. They're big league this
lot, honest.
Eddy What d' y' want me t'do Robbie? Rush off home for me autograph
book?
Robbie (*to the others*) Tch . . . agh . . . come on . . .

They turn and go into the corridor. Eddy follows them

Kav Y' comin' with us Eddy?

Eddy Nah—it's a stag night isn't it? Y' know what y' do on a stag night don't y'?

Kav What Eddy?

Eddy Get pissed!

They exit from the corridor

The Lights come up in the Ladies

Carol (*shouting*) Linda ... are you comin' out?

Linda (*after a pause*) No!

Bernadette Linda ... Linda love ... why not?

Linda Because, Berni love ... you are getting right up my fucking nose!

Carol Linda d'you really think that's appropriate language for a bride-to-be?

Bernadette Take no notice of her Carol ... she doesn't mean it. They all go a bit funny when they're gettin' married. She's probably just havin' a little cry to herself. They do that on the night before.

Carol (*whispering*) Agh yeh. Agh ...

Maureen (*leaning in, joining the whispering*) What?

Carol She's havin' a little cry. Did you Berni, did you cry the night before you got married?

Bernadette No love. I've just been cryin' ever since!

Maureen (*to Frances*) Come here ... Frankie come here ... leave her ... she's just havin' a little cry to herself ... Agh.

Frances Cryin' ... what for?

Maureen Frances! She's crying for what she'll be losing tomorrow.

Frances (*laughing*) Oh 'ey Maureen, she lost that years ago, just like the rest of us.

Maureen No ... I didn't mean that. But y' do give something up when y' get married don't y'? You give up bein' a girl when y' get married.

Frances What d' y' turn into instead—a feller? Her Dave's not gonna be too happy about that tomorrow night is he?

Maureen (*slow*) What?

Frances (*banging on the WC door*) Linda ... come on ... the night's gonna be over.

Maureen Frances ... leave her with her last thoughts as a single girl. Come here. (*Whispering*) What have y' bought for them?

Frances Weddin' presents y' mean?

Maureen Shush! Yeh. I thought I'd go for something functional. I mean it's nice havin' pictures an' ornaments but y' can't do anything with them can you? Apart from look at them!

Bernadette What have y' bought them then Mo?

Maureen (*delighted*) A pair of barbecue chairs! In saddle brown.

Frances (*aghast*) What are they?

Maureen Barbecue chairs. Y' know for in the summer when you have friends round for a barbecue.

Frances Oh that'll be very functional Maureen. They'll have a great time with a barbecue in a block of flats six floors high!

Maureen Oh . . . oh . . . 'ey . . . (*Thinking*) But they will have a balcony won't they?

The others look at each other in disbelief

No . . . I don't mean they'll be able to have a barbecue on the balcony. But they'll be able to sit out there won't they?

Frances An' watch the sun go down on the other blocks of flats!

Maureen I'll tell her that they're balcony chairs. She won't know the difference will she? I'll tell her they're balcony chairs.

Carol We all clubbed together in work. We got them a coffee percolator. Y'know for real coffee.

Bernadette Ah that'll be nice Carol. They'll be able to sit an' have coffee when their friends come round.

Frances Or when they're sittin' out on the balcony! What have you got them Berni?

Bernadette My feller knows someone at work who makes antique furniture, they're great. I've got them a coffee table in antique.

Frances Christ I hope they like coffee! I've got them a coffee set!

Maureen Ah that'll be really swish that, won't it? They will like coffee Frances. You might drink tea when you're at home with your mum, but when you become a couple you drink coffee together. An' that's worked out really lovely hasn't it? Ah . . . just think—they'll be able to sit at Bernadette's coffee table, drinking coffee out of Carol's percolator in the coffee cups that you gave them, sittin' on my balcony chairs. Agh. It'll remind them of us won't it?

Frances They'll never be able to forget us Mo. (*She knocks on the WC door*) Linda!

Bernadette Oh come on Linda love . . . all the good lookin' lads'll have gone home if they think I'm not here.

As they wait for her, the Lights cross-fade to the Gents

We see Robbie and Billy burst through the double doors and into the Gents

Robbie The bitch . . . the stuck-up bitch . . .

Billy (*checking out Dave*) All right Dave. Yeh.

Robbie She was dead fuckin' humpety anyway! She was destroyed when y' got in close.

Robbie I've told you three times haven't I? What d' y' want me t' do, write it out for y'?

Billy But I couldn't hear y' in there, with the music an' that . . . go on, what did she say?

Robbie She said—"I never dance with men in suits."

Billy Is that what she said?

Robbie I thought she was jokin' at first, y'know, comin' on with the laughs an' that. I give her a big smile an' said to her, "I'll tell y' what love, if y' don't like suits why don't we go back t' your place an' y' can take it off for me".

Billy (*laughing*) Did y'? What did she say?
Robbie She walked away. She walked away from me. What's wrong with suits eh? Cost sixty-five quid this did, from Hepworths. No rubbish goes on my back. The stuck-up cow. She doesn't look like Bianca Jagger anyway. She looks more like Mick Jagger. I told her though. Should've heard me Billy . . . classic it was; "Eh love," I said, "I don't waste my time on tarts who don't appreciate quality."
Billy Is that what you said Robbie?
Robbie Too right . . .! "This suit, this suit", I said, "cost every penny of sixty-five notes." See her face did y'? See her face when I told her that?
Billy Yeh Robbie. An' she said "You were robbed."
Robbie (*stung*) I thought you said you couldn't hear!

Eddy enters the corridor

Billy I couldn't hear what you said Robbie. I heard what she said though.
Robbie Well y' wanna get y' friggin' ears tested don't y' 'cos she never said that.
Billy She did Robbie, I was standin'——

Eddy comes in to the Gents

Robbie (*as Eddy enters*) All right Eddy. We were just keepin' an eye on Dave for y'.
Eddy Good lad.
Robbie Doin' y' a favour.
Eddy Yeh . . . Kav's doin' the same for you out there!
Robbie What?
Eddy Know that tart who keeps givin' you the elbow, that really smart-lookin' one, Kav's dancin' with her. She's all over him as well!
Robbie I don't care, I wasn't interested anyway . . . she was destroyed.

Eddy laughs. Robbie heads for the door

Robbie (*to Billy*) Come on.

Robbie and Billy go into the corridor, then exit

Eddy Go on then . . . go on . . . piss off. Piss off t' y' dancin'. An' y' music. Music . . . bleedin' music makes me wanna spew! Eh Dave . . . is that what made you spew, the music eh (*laughing*) music! (*He produces a quarter bottle and takes the cap off*)

The Lights come up in the Ladies. The WC door opens. Linda stands in the door frame

Linda "But if we do not change, tomorrow has no place for us." It says so . . . on the wall in there. (*She goes to the mirror and simply pushes her hair into place*)
Carol Tch. There must have been a students' dance here. No-one with sense'd write somethin' like that.
Maureen They write dead stupid things don't they, students.

Carol I went to a dance once, y'know at the students union. Y' should have seen the bogs, they were full of writin'. An' it was last. Y' couldn't understand any of it. Honest.

Bernadette What was it like?

Carol Y'know all dead soft stuff. Somethin' about God bein' a woman. It was terrible. An' this thing that said "a woman needs a fish like a feller needs a bike" y'know really stupid stuff like that.

Bernadette An' the bloody tax my feller pays to keep them students. Wouldn't y' think with all them brains they'd write somethin' sensible on the bog wall.

Frances Take no notice of her, Berni. There were some really good things. There was this great thing, it said "Love is blind, marriage is an institution, who wants to live in an institute for the blind".

Maureen God Frances ... that's wicked ... don't say things like that.

Linda Come on ... let's go.

Frances You haven't done y' make-up.

Linda I can't be bothered. Come on.

Frances Y' not goin' into a dance without y' make-up on!

Linda Why not?

Bernadette We'll wait for y' Linda ... go on, do y' make-up. Y' don't wanna look a mess.

Frances (*taking Linda's arm*) Come on. I'll do it for y'. Be quicker then.

Linda (*turning away*) Tch. I'll do it meself then. Go on, you lot have waited long enough. Go on, I'll see y' in there. (*She takes out her make-up*)

Carol Linda, we're y' mates aren't we? It's your hen night. Y' don't think we'd desert y' do y'?

Linda Y' not desertin' me. I'll come an' find y' when I'm ready.

Bernadette We never leave someone behind. We only go out when we're all ready.

Carol We stick together.

Linda Why don't y' all come on me honeymoon?

Bernadette We would Linda love, but I'm afraid if I was there, you wouldn't get a look in.

The girls, apart from Linda, laugh

Linda Look ... I am a big girl now y' know. I can find me way out of the Ladies an' into the dance.

Bernadette Linda ... it's your hen night, we stick with you.

Linda Yeh, until some feller wants t' take you outside. Then you'll be off like a flash.

Bernadette Well ... you've got to get a bit of fresh air haven't you?

Linda Is that what you call it?

Bernadette With some of them that's what if feels like!

Shrieks from the girls

Linda Well you'd better watch out tonight, Berni. You're gonna have a bit of competition.

Bernadette Ooh. Tch. Who from?

Linda Well y' don't think I'm gonna end my hen night stuck in the bar like some old married woman do y'? I'm gonna get out on that floor an' forget about everythin' else. I'm gonna get real legless. If it's a last fling then that's what I'm gonna make it.

Frances Well y' better get a move on or your last fling'll be already flung. Come here, let me do it. Go on, you lot go . . . y' can be gettin' the drinks in.

Carol Yeh . . . come on then . . . what y' havin'?

Frances Get us a port an' lemon. What d' y' want, Linda?

Maureen Come on, let's go then.

Linda Get me a pint of bitter.

Bernadette Linda love, now come on. A joke's a joke. I've seen you do that before love and we all think it's a good laugh. But not tonight. It's a hen night you're on, not a stag night. Now come on, something a bit more lady-like.

Linda All right, I'll have a pint of mild!

Bernadette Oh sod off . . .

Carol We'll get y' a Snowball Linda, y'like them.

Linda All right. With a nice little cherry on the top.

Bernadette Come on. We'll be in the bar.

Carol We'll just have a drink an' listen to the sounds till you come out . . .

Bernadette Ogh . . . come on. Give us some music. Music, music, music. It's an aphrodisiac to me.

Linda Bromide'd be an aphrodisiac to you.

Bernadette Too right . . . ooogh . . . come on girls . . .

They go into the corridor and exit

Frances is fixing Linda's hair and make-up

Frances It's great the way music gets to y' though, isn't it? Y' can come to a disco or a dance an' be feelin' really last. But once y' walk into the music it gives y' a lift doesn't it? Makes y' feel special.

Linda Yeh. (*After a pause*) I get lost in music I do.

Frances Yeh I do that.

Linda I become someone else when the music's playin'. I do y' know.

Frances Yeh I'm like that.

Linda D' y' know if it wasn't for music I wouldn't be gettin' married tomorrow.

Frances (*laughing*) Oh don't be stupid Linda. You're nuts sometimes. Y' are y' know.

Linda I'm not bein' stupid. We were dancin' when he asked me to marry him. "When A Man Loves A Woman" it was. I heard this voice in me ear, like it was part of the music, sayin' "Will y' marry me?" So I said yeh. I would've said yeh if I'd been dancin' with Dracula's ugly brother.

Frances Linda stop bein' soft.

Linda When the music stopped I looked up an' there was Dave, beamin' down at me, talkin' about gettin' married an' I'm wonderin' what he's on about, then I remembered. An' the next thing y' know I'm here, tonight.

Frances Linda!

Linda Oh come on, hurry up an' get me hair done. All I wanna do is get out there an' dance the night away. There mightn't be another opportunity after tonight.

Frances Linda, you're gettin' married, not gettin' locked up! There y' go. (*She begins putting her implements away*)

Linda (*looking at herself in the mirror*) Y' do get frightened y' know. I mean if it was just gettin' married to Dave it'd be OK, he's all right Dave is. But it's like, honest, it's like I'm gettin' married to a town.

Frances To a what?

Linda It's not just like I'm marryin' Dave. It's like if I marry him I marry everythin'. Like, I could sit down now an' draw you a chart of everythin' that'll happen in my life after tomorrow.

Frances (*looking at her*) D' y' know something Linda, you're my best mate, but half the time I think you're a looney!

Linda (*going into an exaggerated looney routine*) I am ... (*She plays it up*)

Frances (*laughing*) Linda ... don't mess y' hair up ...

Linda (*quickly knocking her hair back into place, preparing to leave*) Well ... look at it this way, after tomorrow I'll have me own Hoover, me own colour telly an' enough equipment to set up a chain of coffee bars.

They go into the corridor and exit

The Lights come up in the Gents. Eddy is taking a swing from the bottle

Eddy (*laughing*) Ey, Dave ... d' y' wanna drink? (*He laughs*) 'Ey, can't y' hear me Dave? Jesus ... you wouldn't hear if a bomb went off would y'? It's your own fault Dave. Y' can't blame me lad. It's all your own fault. Y' don't have t'drink do y'. See, y' don't have t' do anythin'. (*He pauses*) The US, Dave, an' you coulda' been comin' with me ... you should've been comin' with me. Not with a wife though. Y' can't travel when there's too much baggage weighin' y' down. (*He pauses*) She's OK your tart. She's all right. But round here, if y' get married Dave, y' trapped then. It's the end. Y' don't go anywhere, y' just stay forever in thus fuckin' dyin' dump. It's hard to get out anyway Dave, you know it is. Look at all the scouts who've seen our team. But I'm still here aren't I eh? It's hard to go. But once y' get married round here, y' never gonna go at all. You've got t' fuckin' leave y'self free Dave so that when the time comes y' can be off without a word to anyone. Y've got t' leave y'self free like me. I can go anywhere Dave, anywhere, at any time. There's nothin' holdin' me down. (*He pauses*) But if you don't wanna come with me, if you wanna get married to some tart, well you do it. Yeh you do it mate! Mate? Soft get ...

Robbie and Billy enter from the foyer and go towards the Gents

Eddy goes to take a swig from the bottle. Robbie and Billy enter. Eddy quickly hides the bottle in his pocket. Billy stands at the door. Robbie goes to the urinal

Robbie All right Eddy. (*He sees Billy holding the door*) Come in an' close the bleedin' door will y'?

Billy (*entering*) What have we come in here for? We told them we'd see them in the bar. Yeh.

Robbie Yeh . . . soft lad . . . we told them that 'cos we wanted t' get rid of them didn't we?

Billy Did we? Mine was nice!

Robbie Nice? Shoulda seen her Eddy, she could have had the star part in "Jaws".

Eddy Where's Kav?

Robbie What?

Billy We saw him goin' out the back with that one who looks like Bianca Jagger.

Robbie I hope he gets a dose.

Eddy (*moving to the door*) I'm goin' the bar. (*Snorting*) Soft gets . . .

Billy Are you pissed Eddy?

Eddy (*wheeling and grabbing him*) Have you ever seen me pissed?

Billy No Eddy.

Eddy No Eddy . . . I don't get pissed. I'm not like you. I'm not like him . . . I don't get pissed.

Billy No Eddy, what I meant was——

Robbie Shut up Billy . . .

Eddy Yeh, shut it. Soft arse! (*He pushes him away and goes to the door*) Look after Dave. I'm goin' the bar.

Eddy goes into the corridor and exits

Billy I think he is a bit pissed y'know Robbie.

Robbie Well there's no need to go tellin him is there? Eddy thinks he never gets pissed. I've seen him in a state loads of times. But I never tell him.

Billy Well why doesn't he just say, y' know, that he's pissed?

Robbie I don't know do I? He just likes to pretend, y' go along with him don't y'? It's like he pretends that one day he's gonna play big league football. Y' just go along with him.

Kav enters. Sheepish

Kav I'm sorry Robbie.

Robbie (*all innocence*) What about, Kav? What's up son?

Kav Y' know.

Robbie What? What?

Kav I'm sorry about gettin' off with your little Bianca one. It wasn't my fault though, honest, she was——

Robbie Did you get off with her? Christ y' didn't did y'? Did you hear that Billy?

Kav What? What's wrong?

Robbie Ah no . . . you'll be all right though, y' didn't go outside with her did y'?

Kav Yeh . . . round the back, why?

Robbie Yeh, but y' didn't slip her one did y'?

Kav Yeh . . . she couldn't get out there fast enough.

Robbie Ogh Kav, Kav . . .

Kav What's up?
Robbie Come on Kav. Why d' y' think I gave her the knock back?
Kav What?
Robbie Tommy Stevens told me didn't he? That one who looks like Mick
Jagger's got the clap! Come on Billy . . . those two'll be up in the bar now.
Ogh . . . wanna see these two we've tapped off with Kav, stunners. What
they like Billy?
Billy Y' wanna see them Kav. Ugliest boots y' ever saw in y'——
Robbie Go way soft lad . . . take no notice of him, he's blind.

A coughing from the WC takes them over to Dave

That's it Dave, go on get it up.
Billy It might be a gold clock. Yeh.
Kav Don't y' think we better get him sobered up? It's his stag night isn't it?
Robbie Christ you're considerate all of a sudden aren't y'? I'll bet y' weren't
thinkin' of him when y' were round the back gettin' a dose off that tart.
Kav I haven't got a dose. You were just messin' . . .
Robbie You wait an' see pal. You wait.
Kav Go away. Come on . . . let's try an' make him get it all up.
Robbie Ah leave him. Christ it's not a proper stag night if the groom's
conscious.
Billy It's bad luck if the groom's sober the night before he gets married, yeh.
Robbie That's right that is. Me dad told me. He was sober on his stag night
an' look what happened to him the next day!
Kav What?
Robbie He married me mother! All right, come on, just get him right over
the bowl an' he'll be OK.

*In the corridor Peter enters, carrying a pint. Passing him, carrying cable, is
the Roadie*

Peter Have y' cracked it?
Roadie (*southern accent*) Have we fuck. Every socket we try's an antique.
What a bleedin' dump. Every socket I try just blows.
Peter Keep tryin'.
Roadie I'll keep tryin' but I'm tellin' y' it'll be a miracle if you get on
tonight. What a place. What a fuckin' town.
Peter 'Ey, dickhead, I'll have you know you're talkin' about my home
town.
Roadie Yeh . . . an' I can see why y' left it now. Where y' goin'?
Peter There's no bogs workin' backstage.
Roadie See . . . see what I mean? Will I be glad when this one's over.
Peter Get lost. You'd be moanin' about the state of the plug sockets if we
were playin' the bleedin' Hollywood Bowl.
Roadie I'll tell you what Peter mate, after this place I'll never complain
about a plug socket again.
Peter Well comin' here's done some good then!
Roadie Huh!

The Roadie exits

Peter goes into the Gents, pint in hand, smoking, goes to the urinal. He leans back and looks at what the fellers are doing

Peter All right lads. Christ he's in a state isn't he?

They look at him

What's up with him, one over the eight?

Robbie No, it's his hobby, lookin' down bogs!

Peter (*laughing*) No accountin' for taste eh?

They stand and look at him. He zips up and returns the gaze

Kav 'Ey, d' y' get paid for wearin' boots like that?

Peter What? (*Laughing*) Good aren't they? (*He shows them off*) Like them?

Billy They look like tarts' boots to me.

Peter They are tarts' boots. Good though aren't they?

Robbie (*laughing*) Tarts' boots.

Billy I wouldn't even wear them if I was a tart!

Peter (*walking through them and getting a look at Dave*) What's he been drinkin'?

Robbie (*aggressively*) Y' what?

Peter You deaf?

Robbie What the fuck d' you wanna know what he's been drinkin' for?

Peter It's one of me hobbies, gettin' to know what people drink.

Billy He's been on Black Velvets an' Southern Comfort.

Peter Ah. That type is he? Subtle palate?

Kav Listen you— who the fuck d' y' think you're talkin' to?

Peter Kavanagh isn't it? Erm ... Tony Kavanagh.

Kav How the fuck d' you know my name? How does he know my name? Listen you, you just ... (*Pointing*) Hold on ... ey ... it is, isn't it it is! You used to live round our way didn't y'?

Robbie Ogh fuck. It's you isn't it?

Peter I hope so.

Billy Who is it?

Kav (*excited*) You know ... you know him ... er hold on, hold on, don't tell me ... it's erm ... erm.

Peter Peter ...

Kav That's it, that's it ... I knew it was ...

Robbie 'Ey, you're famous aren't y'?

Kav Are you with this group tonight? 'Ey ... they're famous ...

Billy Who is it?

Kav 'Ey ... I always said you were dead good on that guitar y' know, I did didn't I Robbie? Here, look, that's Robbie. Y' remember Robbie don't y'?

Peter Hia Robbie.

Kav An' Billy ... y' remember Billy don't y', Billy Blake?

Peter Erm ...

Kav Ah y' do ... y' must do ... his mam an' your mam were mates ... remember ...

Peter Oh yeh ... all right erm ...

Billy Who is he?

Kav Christ, is that really you? Look at y' now! An' you used to be just like us! Tch. 'Ey, here's Dave. Y' remember Dave don't y'? (*He leads him over*)
Peter Er, no I think er . . .
Kav Ah y' do. You remember Dave. (*Shouting*) 'Ey Dave, Dave, wake up . . . look who's here Dave! Dave'll be sick at missin' y'.
Peter Maybe that's the best thing eh?
Kav (*laughing, too much*) Still kept your sense of humour eh? Great. (*He looks at him*) I can't believe it.
Robbie What y' doin' playin' in a dump like this?
Peter It's work isn't it?
Kav (*to anyone*) Gis a piece of paper, where's a piece of paper? (*He goes into the WC*)
Robbie You're on the radio an' the telly an that, aren't y'?
Peter Now an' then.
Robbie An' y' come back playin' in dives like this.
Peter It's only one gig. It was arranged before the single happened.
Robbie Well y' should've told them to fuck off. Y' don't wanna belittle y'selves do y', playin' holes like this when y' famous. Live in London now do y'?
Peter Yeh.
Robbie What's it like?
Peter It's all right man, it's OK.
Robbie (*looking at him*) I'll bet it's fuckin' great!
Peter (*smiling*) It's OK.
Robbie (*looking at him*) Jesus!
Peter Small world eh?
Kav (*coming out of the WC with bog paper*) I'm sorry about the paper, I couldn't find any other . . . (*He offers pencil and paper*)
Peter Ah come on man, you don't want . . .
Kav Put, erm . . . "To Kav—an old mate".
Peter Look man, for Christ's sake you don't want me to do this . . .
Kav You're jokin' aren't y'? Of course I do . . .
Peter Look, for Christ's sake I used to live just down the road from you . . .
Kav I know. I'm gonna show that to people.

Peter looks at him. Billy comes out of the WC with a piece of paper, joins the queue. Peter signs

Robbie 'Ey is it true what they say about the tarts, y' know, the groupies.
Peter A bit of it. Most of it's fiction.
Robbie I'll bet it's not. Jesus I bet you can have anythin' y' want can't y'?
Kav (*looking at his piece of paper*) Ogh . . . look at that!

Peter takes Billy's paper, signs it

Robbie 'Ey, what sort of a car d' y' drive now?
Peter I haven't got one. Listen, what you lads doin' these days?
Robbie Fuck all, us. Eh, have y' got a big house in London?
Peter A flat. What, y' all on the dole?
Kav Nah, we work.

Robbie Got a big house in the country have y'?
Peter What sort of work's that then?
Kav Listen, we don't wanna talk about us, it's dead borin'. We just fuckin'
work. Go on, tell us all about you. Tell us all about the, y' know, the
thingy, an, what it's like an' all about it.
Peter Go way. What d' y' wanna hear about me for?
Kav Listen Peter. You're someone who's made it. We're proud of you. We
are.

Billy has been studying his piece of bog paper

Billy Who is he?
Robbie Can't you read?
Peter Look lads . . . I've gorra go. We haven't even got the gear set up yet.
Gotta tune up an' that . . .
Robbie Aren't y' gonna come an' have a bevvy with us?
Peter We're not even set up yet.
Kav What about afterwards, y' know after the gig?
Peter Yeh, maybe . . . that's a possibility. See y' lads. 'Ey, look after the
Southern Comfort King won't y'?

He goes into the corridor and exits

Kav See y' Peter.
Robbie Tarar.
Billy (*looking up from his paper*) 'Ey . . . that was Peter Taylor! Ogh . . . he's
famous. Yeh.
Robbie Imagine comin' back to this dive when y' as big as he is. See his
boots. They were smart weren't they?
Billy I'm gonna get a pair of them.
Robbie They wouldn't look the same on you.
Billy Why won't they?
Robbie They just won't.
Kav They'll be custom-made anyway.
Robbie Y' wouldn't get nothin' like that round here.
Kav Christ . . . the way he must live eh?
Robbie I'll bet his tarts never grow old, do they?
Billy Boots like that'd suit me.
Kav I'll bet he's never bored is he? An' he used t' live near us!

Eddy enters

Eddy . . . Eddy guess what?
Eddy I know! Dave's tart's out there!
Others What?
Eddy I've just seen her now. She's out there, dancin'!

BLACK-OUT

ACT II

Bernadette and Carol, laughing, enter the Ladies

Bernadette Ogh ... God! Did y' see the state of him. An' he was serious. He tried to get off with me! He was all of four foot nothin'.

Carol What about his mate? He was smaller. An' he had acne. (*Disgusted*) Oogh, God the thought; four foot nothin' an' spotted all over. He was like a walkin' Eccles cake. Oogh ...

Bernadette At least you got rid of him after the first dance.

Carol I had to Berni. He made me feel ill, honest I hate ugly people. I feel sorry for them like, but no, I had to get rid of him. You should have given yours the elbow straight away.

Bernadette Didn't y' see me tryin'? "Are you stayin' up?" he says to me. All three foot six of him starin' up at me. I said "I don't know about stayin' up, don't y' think y' better sit down before y' get trodden on."

Carol (*shrieking*) Y' didn't ... Berni ... Y' could have hurt his feelings.

Bernadette Y' jokin'. He didn't have any feelings. He just ignored everythin'. He wouldn't take no for an answer. I said to him, "Look son, I'll let y' into a secret, it's no use tryin' it on with me, I'm a lesbian ..."

Carol Berni ...

Bernadette It did no good. "That's all right", he said, "I like a challenge." By this time I'm dancin' away again, hopin' no-one'd see me with him. And honest to God, he's so small he kept gettin' lost. I'm just walkin' away when he appears again. "Goin' for a drink are we?" he says, I said to him, "'Ey you'd better run along, Snow White'll be lookin' for you." Ey, he didn't get it though. "Oh I'm sorry", I said, "but I thought you were one of the Seven Dwarfs." He started laughin' then, y' know, makin' out he's got a sense of humour. "Oh yeh", he says, "I'm Dozy," I said "You're not friggin' kiddin' ..."

Carol and Bernadette laugh

I'm walkin' away an' he's shoutin after me "'Ey I'll see y' in the bar, I'll be in the bar." I said "Yeh, an' that's the best place for you, along with every other pint that thinks it's a quart!"

Frances enters

Carol Frankie ... have y' been in the bar?

Frances Yeh.

Carol Is there a spotted midget in there?

Frances Ogh him? He's destroyed isn't he? An' his mate, just been tryin' to chat me up.

Bernadette Well the two-timin' sod!

Frances Three-timin'. He's chattin' Mo up now.

Carol Ogh God.

Frances She's made up!

Carol Go way!

Frances She's just standin' there, beamin' down at him with big dreamy eyes. Mind you that might be the Pernod. She's had five in the last half-hour.

Bernadette She'll need a bottle full if she's takin' him on.

Maureen, well away, enters. She's singing the chorus of "Dancing Queen"

Maureen Whoa . . . hia . . . I feel great! . . . great! That's how I feel . . . great . . . I feel really . . . beautiful . . .

Frances I thought you were off with someone.

Maureen (*laughing*) Big John Wayne . . .!

Frances I thought it was all set up Maureen.

Maureen He said, he did, he said to me . . . "D' y' wanna drink?" So, so I said, "Yeh, a double Pernod!"

Carol Tch. Maureen!

Maureen He said, "On y' bike." "On y' bike", he said, "y' can have half a lager an' like it." Honest, cheeky get; he said "I'm not made of money y' know." So I said (*laughing*) an' I was dead made up with this, I said to him, "Listen you, to make you out of money would only cost about three an' a half pence!" (*Laughing*) An' he got all dead narked then, an' said he was fed up 'cos people had been takin' the piss all night. So y' know what I said, I told him to go for a swim in his half of lager!

She laughs and goes into the song again. Raucous, pitched too high. The others join in.

Linda enters. She joins in the singing

We're havin' a good time, aren't we? Aren't we eh? We're all havin' another good time. Ogh sometimes . . . sometimes I feel so happy. Linda . . . Linda, are you havin' a good time?

Linda Great Mo.

Frances God, can't y' tell she is? Haven't y' seen her, she hasn't stopped dancin' since she got out there . . . have y' Linda?

Linda I love this y' know. I love it when we're all out together an' havin' a laugh. It's good isn't it? It's great.

Bernadette Y' can't beat it when there's a crowd of y'.

Linda Come on . . . let's all go out an' have a dance together . . .

Frances Come on yeh, we'll have a line out . . .

Carol Agh yeh . . .

Linda An' if any fellers try to split us up we'll tell them to sod off . . .

Frances (*as she leaves*) Come on . . .

Maureen (*as she leaves*) I feel a bit sick . . .

Bernadette Come on . . . (*Pushing Maureen*) Get out . . . you'll be all right . . .

They all go down the corridor. Someone begins the "Dancing Queen" chorus, they all sing

The Lights come up in the Gents. The fellers are all as at the end of Act I

Eddy Talk about a rope round y' neck . . .

Kav Yeh, but what I'm tryin' to tell y' Eddy is who's been *here*!

Eddy She's not even married to him yet, an' she's spyin' on him! Couldn't she leave him alone eh? Couldn't she leave him with his mates on his last night?

Kav Eddy . . .

Robbie She won't know Dave's here Eddy. She'll just be here for the dancin'.

Kav Eddy guess——

Eddy Dancin', yeh, she's dancin' all right. I just seen her from the balcony, dancin' round with all different fellers, the bitch!

Robbie Come on Eddy, it's only dancin'.

Eddy Is it? An' what about him? (*He indicates Dave*)

Robbie Christ Eddy, she's only dancin', isn't she?

Kav Forget her Eddy . . . listen, y' know who's been here eh? Guess who's been standin' on that very spot you're standin' on.

Billy Y' should've seen his boots Eddy. Custom-made, yeh.

Kav Go on Eddy, guess, guess who?

Eddy I don't fuckin' know do I?

Kav Peter Taylor!

Eddy Who?

Kav You know Peter Taylor. Remember? He used to live round our way, played the guitar. He's with this group that's on tonight. He's famous Eddy.

Eddy Famous?

Billy He's got these great boots Eddy. I'm gonna get a pair. Yeh.

Kav You'll be able to see him after Eddy. He's gonna have a drink with us, y' know after the gig.

Eddy After the what?

Kav The gig. That's what they call it Eddy, when they play somewhere.

Billy He's a real star y' know Eddy.

Eddy I thought I told you to look after Dave.

Billy We have done Eddy.

Robbie (*to Dave*) All right Dave? OK?

Billy (*going across to join Robbie*) All right Dave? Yeh.

Kav Ah he's fantastic Eddy, not stuck up or anythin' y' know. (*He brings out his autograph*) Look Eddy.

Eddy takes it

See what it says Eddy . . . "To Kav— an old mate" an' that's his name there.

Billy (*coming over with his autograph paper*) He did one for me Eddy, look. Yeh.

Eddy takes it and looks at it

I'll bet he'll do one for you Eddy. Yeh. If y' ask him.

Eddy What are these?

Billy Yeh, it's dead hard to read at first Eddy, I couldn't read it at first but look it says . . .

He goes to point at the paper. Eddy turns away, holding up the paper

Eddy This? What's this?
Billy We didn't have an autograph book Eddy.
Eddy You big soft tarts!
Kav What Eddy?
Eddy Kids get autographs. Are you little kids?
Kav No Eddy, but he's famous!
Eddy On y' bike! (*He crumples up the paper*) Famous!

He goes to the WC, throws the paper down the pan and flushes it

Kav (*transfixed*) Eddy, what have y' done?
Eddy (*coming out*) What have I done?
Robbie (*from the bog*) You've just flushed Dave's head, Eddy.
Eddy Do it again. It might sober him up.
Kav Eddy! That was my autograph!
Billy An' mine. But y' couldn't read it anyway.
Kav Eddy, that was my fuckin' autograph!
Eddy (*swiftly grabbing him*) Who the fuck d' y'think you're talking to? (*He glares him into submission*) Y'don't get autographs from people like him! He's just a fuckin' nomark!

He glares at Kav who stares back, helpless. Eddy lets him go

Y'don't wanna waste y'time Kav. See, it's people like you Kav, runnin' around after people like him that make them what they are. You're as good as he is! Did he ask you for your autograph? Did he?
Kav (*quietly*) No.
Eddy No. You wanna keep your dignity you do. You're good as him. You could do that, what he does if you wanted to. You can do anythin' he can do. We all can. We can do anythin' we want to do, anythin'. He's nothin' special, so don't belittle y'self beggin' for a scrawlin' on a piece of bog paper. We can all write our names y' know. Here, here, give me that pencil. Give it me!

Kav does so

Look, look, it's dead easy y' know. You want an autograph? I'll give y' a fuckin' autograph . . . here. (*He writes his name in huge letters on the wall*)
Kav It was great meetin' him though. Wasn't it Robbie?
Robbie It was all right.
Billy Gis a go Eddy, Eddy . . . I'm gonna do my autograph. I am. I'm gonna do mine bigger than yours Eddy. Yeh.
Robbie He's no bleedin' big shot is he? Hasn't even got a car.
Billy (*doing his name*) Y' shoulda seen the stupid boots he had on Eddy, y' know, tarts' boots.
Robbie (*taking out a felt-tip pen and doing his own name*) He's nothin' special, anyone could do what he does.
Kav Oh yeh. Anyone could do it. That's why later on, while he's standin' up on the stage with all the coloured spotlights on him, you'll be down on the floor, dancin' in the dark with all the other nomarks.

. .

Eddy (*snatching the pencil from Billy*) Gis that. (*He offers it to Kav*) Go on!
Kav What?
Eddy Put y' name up.
Kav (*after a pause*) I don't want to Eddy.
Eddy Why?
Kav There's no point is there?
Eddy The point, Kav, is that our names are up there. Where's yours?
Kav What?
Eddy Your name has got to be up there!
Kav Why?
Eddy So they can be seen, that's why. So that everyone'll know we've been here.
Kav They'll only paint it out. They always do.
Eddy Let them, we'll come back an' do it again.
Kav Then they'll stipple over the walls so y' can't write on them.
Eddy So. We'll come back again, an' carve our names out, won't we? I've told y' Kav, we can do anythin'. (*He pauses*) Write y' name.

Kav looks at Eddy

Robbie Go on Kav. I wouldn't mind, but he can write better than any of us.
Eddy Come on Kav. I want y' t' do it for me. Y' know the way y' do it in fancy scrolls an' that, that's clever that is Kav. You do it. For us. Come on.
Kav (*taking the pencil; after a pause*) All right Eddy.
Eddy Agh . . . good lad Kav.
Kav (*stepping up to the wall, looking at their writings*) Who taught you lot t' write? Look at the state of that.
Eddy You show us how it should be done Kav.
Kav (*beginning to write*) Go on, you'se lot go. It'll take a bit of time this. Go on, I can keep me eye on Dave, Eddy.
Eddy Come on . . . (*He goes into the corridor*)
Robbie (*following with Billy*) Y' gonna go for a dance Eddy?
Eddy Nah.
Billy Why not Eddy?
Eddy 'Cos I'd rather just watch youse make fools of yourselves.

They exit

As Kav is doing his name, we see Bernadette and Carol, followed by Maureen, come through the doors

Bernadette Well the inconsiderate swines.
Carol Tch.
Maureen What's up?
Carol (*as they enter the Ladies*) You saw them didn't y'?
Maureen Who? Oh me head . . .
Carol Robbie Smith's here. An' Billy Blake.
Maureen Oh he's nice him, Billy Blake isn't he?
Carol Tch. God Maureen, that's not the point is it?
Maureen What?

Bernadette Maureen love, if Billy Blake an' Robbie Smith an' them are here, who else must be here?

Maureen Dave! Dave? Oh God . . . get Linda in, get Linda in here quick . . .

Carol (*pulling her back from the door*) Come here, Frances has gone to tell her . . .

Bernadette We'll just have t' go somewhere else.

Carol Tch. I was dead made up when I first saw Robbie, I really fancy him.

Bernadette Fancy him or not Carol, we can't take the risk, for Linda's sake.

Carol Oh God I know, I'm not sayin' we should take the risk, Berni.

Maureen If she sees her Dave tonight that's it y' know. Her marriage has had it.

Bernadette We'll go somewhere else. We'll have to.

Maureen My Mum knew a couple who saw each other the night before they got married an' y' know what happened eh?

Bernadette What?

Maureen The next day, in church, they were standin' y' know in the archway, havin' their picture taken. And the archway collapsed on them. Killed outright, an' that's true that.

Carol That was in the paper wasn't it?

Maureen Yeh, the picture was in the paper wasn't it? Y' know, just a pile of stones, Berni.

Bernadette There was this woman by us y' know, she got an emerald engagement ring . . .

Carol Go way . . .

Maureen Did she take it off for the weddin'?

Bernadette Everyone told her . . .

Carol Y' should never wear green at a weddin' should y'?

Bernadette Everyone told her. But she wouldn't listen, thought she knew best, that type y'know, thought she could make her own rules . . .

Carol Y' can't can y'?

Bernadette He got drowned didn't he, her husband, got drowned on their honeymoon.

Carol Agh go way . . .

Bernadette 'Ey she wouldn't learn though, Carol. A couple of years later she got married again, an' y' know what colour her dress was?

Carol Green?

Maureen Tch . . .

Bernadette Everyone told her. I believe her mother was distraught about it. But she wouldn't listen, tried to make out that things like that didn't matter.

Maureen What happened Berni?

Bernadette Heart attack wasn't it? Three months married an' her feller had a cardiac arrest. Gone, finished!

Carol I'll bet she was sorry after that . . .

Bernadette No, that's not the end of it. She got married again didn't she?

Carol God, y' wouldn't think a feller'd take a chance on her, would y'?

Bernadette She was told, time an' time again she was told, everyone told her. An' she said all right, y'know no green this time . . .

Carol I'll bet her feller was relieved wasn't he?

Bernadette They get to the church an' she hasn't got a patch of green, anywhere.

Maureen Oh thank God for that! Did they live, y' know, happily an' that?

Bernadette Yeh, for ten minutes. As she was walkin' out the church she slipped, knocked her head on one of the gravestones. Dead!

Carol Go way.

Maureen But there was no green, Berni.

Bernadette No, there was no green Mo, but as they picked her up, what did they see? Pinned to her dress?

Maureen What?

Bernadette An opal brooch!

Maureen Agh . . .!

Linda enters, led by Frances. They head for the Ladies

Carol Tch, when y' think about it, gettin' married's a terrible liability y' know.

Maureen Never wear an' opal unless it's y' birth-stone.

Carol She was askin' for trouble though, that one, wasn't she, Berni?

Bernadette Thought it didn't matter y' see. Thought she could make up her own rules.

Linda and Frances enter

Linda For Christ's sake Frances. What's wrong with you lot? If y' wanted to talk to me why didn't y' come out there? Come on, I wanna get back t' the dancin'.

Bernadette Linda love, we've got to go somewhere else.

Linda What's wrong with here?

Carol Give us y' cloakroom tickets, I'll go 'n get the coats an' make sure it's all clear.

Linda What's wrong?

Bernadette Nothing. Apart from the fact that the man you're marryin' is here tonight.

Linda Who? Dave? Where?

Frances He's here, somewhere. We've seen all his mates.

Linda Well?

Bernadette Well what?

Linda Well why do we have to go?

Bernadette Linda! You cannot see your future husband on the eve of your wedding!

Linda Who says so?

Carol Linda, you see your Dave tonight an' your marriage is doomed.

Linda Ogh . . . Carol. Get lost will y' . . .

Maureen Linda, d' you want to end up under a pile of stones.

Linda (*laughing*) What?

Bernadette We don't want to go Linda. This is for your sake love. We're only thinkin' of you Linda.

Carol You can't afford to see Dave tonight, Linda.

Linda Y' don't really believe that do y'?

Carol Linda. Y've got to believe it, 'cos it's true.

Linda Y' do don't y'? You really believe it.

Bernadette Yes, an' so should you. Now come on, let's have your cloak-room ticket, we'll get the coats an'——

Linda (*to Frances*) You don't believe this do y'? Eh?

Frances Well y' don't do y' Linda? Y' don't see each other the night before y' get married.

Linda For Christ's sake. Come on!

Bernadette Linda, we don't want to see you put your future in jeopardy.

Linda (*looking at them; after a pause*) If it wasn't for the fact that you're my mates, an' have been for a long time, I'd say you were all certifiable! (*She stares at them*) Why don't y' do what y' want t' do? Why don't y' do what you think you should do? But y' won't will y'? That's the biggest sin of all to you lot isn't it? You'll just keep on doin' what you're told to, won't y'?

Bernadette Nobody tells me what to do Linda. I do whatever I want to do.

Linda Oh do y'? Well look Berni, you came here tonight to get off with a feller. Well there's loads of them out there. Come on, come on out an' get one . . .

Bernadette I could do Linda. I could. But for your sake——

Linda For my sake? Look, just forget about my sake, will y'? (*She opens the door*) Now come on, all of y'come on, now . . .

She holds the door for them. They make no move

Well, sod off then! (*She turns and goes out. In the corridor she leans against the wall, takes out her cigarettes, lights one*)

Bernadette Well if you ask me I say she's not been herself all night.

Frances But that's what she's like Berni. How long have I been her mate eh? An' I've seen her, she can be like this y' know . . .

Bernadette It's the pressure isn't it? I know what's goin' through her mind.

Carol Yeh but if she's actin' like this now Berni, imagine what she'll be like tomorrow.

Bernadette What we've got to do is to stop her doin' anythin' stupid, whether she wants to or not.

Frances I say we go an' see the fellers. Tell them to go somewhere else.

Carol They won't though will they? Y' know what fellers are like.

Frances We were here first weren't we? So it. I'll go an' see if I can find Eddy Ainsworth. He'll tell them what to do. If he says leave they will do.

Frances goes out to the corridor. In the Ladies they pass around fags, smoking, thinking, as the Lights fade. In the corridor . . .

Linda (*as Frances passes*) Frances . . .

Frances tries to ignore it

Frankie . . .!

Frances (*turning*) What?

Linda (*after a pause*) Forget it.

Frances Listen Linda . . . I don't know what's wrong with you tonight but you can't half be an awkward bitch . . .

Linda turns away

Frances continues on down the corridor and out through the doors

From the other end of the corridor we see Peter and the Roadie enter

Roadie Well I'll try this and I'm tellin' y', if it don't work we've had it. We might as well throw the gear back in the van an' piss off.
Peter Not play at all?

Linda looks up, with recognition

Roadie Well y' can't play without power can y'? You show me how t' get some power out to the——
Linda Hello . . .
Roadie (*thinking it's for him*) Hello darlin', what y' doin' eh?
Linda (*passing him*) 'Ey.
Peter (*looking at her, with recognition*) Christ! 'Ey . . . Jesus . . . come here . . .

He hugs her, she breaks away smiling and looking at him

Roadie (*going down the corridor*) What the fuck. I wish I was famous . . .

He exits

Linda (*looking at him*) Well the state of you!
Peter What d' y' mean?

The Roadie sticks his head through the doors

Roadie 'Ey . . . an' don't be long. You're on in a minute . . .
Peter I thought you said y' couldn't get any power!
Roadie I will now!

The Roadie exits

Peter (*of his gear*) Like it do y'?
Linda Where d' y' get y' boots?
Peter (*camp*) Tch. Chelsea Girl . . .
Linda (*laughing*) They're great . . .
Peter Did y' know we were on?
Linda No. How long have y' been with this lot?
Peter 'Bout a year. Just out for a bop are y'?
Linda Sort of.
Peter Christ, I would have thought you'd given up comin' to this sort of place.
Linda Same could be said for you.
Peter Nah . . . it's different for me isn't it? I'll never grow up.

She laughs

Anyway, it's work isn't it? I don't come out of choice. (*He laughs*) How are y'?
Linda All right. How are you?
Peter I'm OK. Lovely. Tch. I'm all right.

Taylor. An' him an' Linda only had a thing goin' for about two years didn't they?

Carol You what?

Frances They're right outside this door, now, arms round each other . . .

Bernadette Oh . . . so that's why she wanted to come here is it.

Frances Well we don't know that, Berni . . .

Carol Oh come off it, Frances . . .

Bernadette Look Frances, if she went out with him for that long she's bound t' know what group he's playin' in . . . there's a poster outside isn't there?

Carol I wondered why Linda wanted to come to a dump like this. Well fancy doin' somethin' like this, on y' weddin' night . . .

Maureen God . . . no good'll come of this . . . I'm tellin' y' I know . . .

Frances Look . . . she is only talkin' to him . . .

Bernadette Yes, an' we all know where talk leads . . .

Maureen Don't Berni . . . don't . . .

Carol Y' don't see ex fellers the night before y' gettin' married do y'?

Frances She could just have bumped into him y' know . . .

Bernadette Well we can soon find out can't we Frances? Well get her in here . . . (*She goes out to the corridor*)

Frances (*sighing*) Ogh Christ . . .

Carol I knew we shoulda gone the Top Rank . . . I knew we shouldn't have come here.

Bernadette comes in

Bernadette Where did you say she was?

Frances Just outside.

Bernadette Well she's not there now . . .

Carol Well where is she?

Bernadette How do I know? But I'll tell y' what, if y' ask me she's up to no good. That girl is playin' with fire. We're her mates, I reckon we better sort out a way to stop her gettin' burnt . . .

Maureen Oh God . . . (*Beginning to cry, she rushes into the WC*)

Frances For God's sake Maureen shut it will y' . . .

Maureen (*frantic*) Why can't everything be nice?

Bernadette Who said everything won't be nice Maureen?

Maureen (*crying*) No good'll come of this . . . You mark my words . . . you see . . .

Bernadette Maureen . . . we'll sort it out, don't worry. Everything will be nice Maureen. There's a wedding tomorrow; there'll be a nice cake and a nice service, nice bridesmaids, nice presents. And a nice bride and groom. But Mo, we've just got to see that Linda doesn't do anything silly. We're her mates Mo. What are mates for eh? Eh?

Maureen comes out of the WC. Bernadette puts her arm round her

Everything will be nice love. We'll look after her . . . don't worry. Come on . . . everything'll be very nice.

The girls go into the corridor as . . .

Linda (*looking at him*) The state of y'.
Peter I thought y' liked it.
Linda I do but y' don't wanna go out like that round here. Y'll get locke
up.
Peter I know. We went over the road for a pint before. Should have hear
them in there . . . "All right cowboy" they kept shoutin'. "Where's Tont
then?" (*He laughs*) I dunno . . .
Linda Well what d' y' expect if y' come round here in women's boots?
Peter (*grabbing her in a mock headlock*) Agh . . . (*He turns it into a hug*) Yo
know better than that. (*He holds her and looks at her. Shaking his head*)
can't believe it.

Frances comes through the corridor doors

*Linda pulls away from him. Frances clocks it. She goes into the loo, closes the
door, leans on it*

Peter Isn't that whatshecalled, your mate?
Linda Frances.
Peter Frances, that's right. How is she?
Linda All right.
Peter 'Ey it's great to see y' y' know.
Linda It's great to see you. I suppose.
Peter Suppose? Tch. I'll say tarar an' go an' tune up if you like.
Linda Go on then.
Peter Come off it. Fancy a dance?
Linda With you?
Peter No, with Tonto! Who d' y' think?
Linda I didn't think fellers from famous groups went dancin', I thought
they kept themselves apart from the rabble.
Peter They do usually. But you're special rabble!
Linda Tch. Oh such flattery. Or was it an insult?
Peter (*leading her along the corridor*) Come on. What's the dance up here
these days? Still do the twist?
Linda The Foxtrot actually . . .
Peter Oh is it actually . . .

They go through the doors

Frances moves from the outer door, through the inner door into the Ladies

Carol What did they say?
Bernadette Well?
Carol Are they goin' Fran?
Frances No.
Carol Tch. Fellers.
Frances Listen. Guess whose group it is that's playin'?
Bernadette Y' what?
Frances Peter Taylor. It's his group . . .
Bernadette We don't wanna know about a group Frances, we wanna
know——
Frances Berni! The thing is Berni, in this group there's a feller called Peter

Billy and Robbie come through the doors

Robbie All right girls?
Bernadette Come on girls . . .
Carol (*stopping*) Hia Robbie . . .
Robbie All right . . . er . . . Carol isn't it?
Carol (*flattered*) Tch . . . y' good at names aren't y'?
Robbie I'm good at most things Carol!
Bernadette (*from the door*) CAROL!
Carol Got t' go. See y' tomorrow eh Robbie . . . at the weddin' . . .

She dashes off through doors, following the others

Billy You're on there Robbie. I could tell. Yeh . . .
Robbie Don't fancy it much though . . .
Billy Don't y'?
Robbie Nah. I'd screw it though. Come on . . . hurry up or them other two'll have gone.

As they are entering the Gents, the Lights come up

'Ey they're crackers those two aren't they?
Billy Yours is Robbie. Yeh . . .
Robbie Dead ringer for Britt Ekland isn't she? Whoa. Come on . . .

They enter the Gents. Kav is putting the finishing touches to an impressive drawing of his own name

Ogh . . . look at that . . .
Billy That's dead smart that Kav.
Kav It's all right isn't it?
Robbie Yeh. 'Ey . . . y' wanna see these two we've tapped off with. Mine looks just like Britt Ekland, doesn't she Billy?
Billy Yeh. Mine looks just like Rod Stewart. That's great that, Kav . . .
Robbie Come on Billy . . . what y' moanin' for? She's all right that one. Don't you go doin' a bunk on her will y'? I'm knackered with the Britt Ekland one if you give her mate the elbow.
Billy I can't stand her though, Robbie. That's smart, Kav.
Robbie What's wrong with her?
Billy She's destroyed.
Robbie Well it's dark in there isn't it? Keep her out the light an' no-one'll notice her hunch back. Ah come on Billy . . . I'd do the same for you wouldn't I eh? Wouldn't I Kav? I'm your mate aren't I?
Billy Yeh.
Robbie Well, I'm askin' y' to do me a favour.
Kav Robbie's right y' know Billy. You stand by y' mates an' they stand by you, don't they?

We see Maureen, Carol and Frances come through the corridor doors and into the Ladies. Bernadette follows them

Billy Yeh. All right.

Robbie Good lad ... come on ... 'ey, it's smart that Kav. Eddy'll be made up with y'.

Kav (*as they leave*) Yeh ... I'm gonna tell him.

Bernadette enters the Ladies just before the fellers come into the corridor and exit

Bernadette Well the brazen ... ogh ... did you see it ... did y' see it?

Maureen Dancin' ... like that, with him ...

Frances An' ignored her mates.

Maureen She was dancin' like she was stuck to him wasn't she?

Bernadette She's makin' a spectacle of herself she is.

Carol An' it wasn't even a slowy was it?

Bernadette Y' don't dance like that to a fast record unless you've got one thing in mind. It's written all over them what they've got in mind.

Maureen What Berni?

Bernadette Come on Maureen. It's patently obvious ...

Carol God, he's got a cheek that feller hasn't he eh, comin' round here, dancin' like that. He must have no shame that feller.

Linda enters through the corridor doors and heads for the Ladies

Bernadette Well I think she's immoral, I do. There's no excuse for that sort of behaviour. Not on the night before y' gettin'——

Linda enters. Immediate silence. She walks through them and into the WC, closing the door

Linda ... Linda!

Linda (*from the WC*) What Berni?

Bernadette Linda, don't y' think you're bein' a bit inconsiderate?

Linda (*all sweetness*) Why's that Bern?

Bernadette I could say "improper" Linda, but I won't. There is moderation y' know Linda.

Linda (*from the WC*) Why don't y' tell me what's botherin' y' Bern?

Bernadette Do you really think you should be carrying on like this, with a stranger, the night before your wedding?

Linda (*from the WC*) He's not a stranger ... he's someone I know very well. You could call him an intimate friend Berni ...

Bernadette Don't you try and take the piss out of me Linda.

The WC flushes, the door opens and Linda crosses to the basin

Linda Berni ... I'm dancing, that's all.

Carol Yeh, but y' used to go out with him didn't y' Linda?

Linda Yes Carol, I did.

Carol Well don't y' think that makes it worse?

Linda (*drying her hands*) No Carol, I don't think it makes it anything. I am dancin', with someone I used to go out with. I like him. I like him very much as it happens. An' I think it's got sod all to do with you, or you or you or any of you.

Bernadette Have you forgotten that tomorrow you an' Dave will be standing in that church, getting married?

She finishes drying her hands, goes to the door, opens it, turns and looks at them

Linda An' what makes you think I'm still going ahead with it?

Linda goes into the corridor and exits

Maureen I knew it ... I told you ... I knew it ... what did I say?

Carol God, I'm supposed to be a bridesmaid an' everything' ...

Maureen I'm gonna be sick, I am, I'm gonna be sick. What am I gonna do with the barbecue chairs?

Bernadette This is gettin' out of hand this is.

Frances What we gonna do?

Bernadette Y' know who y' can blame for this don't y', eh? This is Peter Whatsisname's doing isn't it?

Carol What we gonna do though Berni?

Bernadette Well if y' ask me Carol I reckon the sooner she gets away from that Peter feller and comes to her senses the better it'll be for everyone.

Frances She's makin' a fool of herself.

Bernadette She's makin' a fool of everyone. I think the fellers should know about this. I think they've got to be told ...

Carol Don't tell Dave, Berni ...

Bernadette I won't have to tell him if she carries on flauntin' herself out there. He'll see it for himself soon enough. No, come on, we'll tell the others ...

They begin to exit into the corridor

Frances What y' gonna say Berni?

Bernadette I'll tell them what she told us ... that the weddin's off!

They go into the corridor and exit through the doors

Peter and Linda enter as if from the bandroom. Peter is carrying a pint

Linda Does that mean you won't be able to play?

Peter Doesn't look like it.

Linda Ah I was lookin' forward t' seein' y'.

Peter It's not our fault. All the wiring's lethal. Every time they connect to a socket it blows. The place is fallin' to bits.

Linda It's like everythin' else round here. It's dyin' this place is. Didn't y' notice?

Peter Huh. I didn't think I'd see y' y' know. I thought you would have left by now.

Linda Left for where?

Peter Nowhere in particular. I just didn't think you'd stay round here.

Linda An' what's wrong with round here?

Peter Come on, y' just said yourself it's dyin'.

Linda Well, that's no reason to leave is it?

Peter I just never thought this place'd be big enough for you.
Linda Get lost!
Peter (*laughing*) I'm not takin' the piss, honest. I'm serious.
Linda Tch.
Peter You should've come to London when I went. You should've come
with me.
Linda I couldn't, could I?
Peter Wouldn't.
Linda All right, wouldn't.
Peter Why?
Linda I didn't (*camping it*) erm, love you enough. (*After a pause*) I didn't
half like you a lot though.
Peter (*camping it*) You always were a smooth-talking bitch Linda.

She smiles

Anyway, I didn't necessarily mean with me in that sense. What y'gonna
do then, settle down here?
Linda I might.
Peter (*shaking his head*) Tch.
Linda 'Ey, it might have escaped your notice but there are a lot of people
who like livin' in this town.
Peter Including you?
Linda Yes.
Peter Why?
Linda Oh sod off you. Just 'cos you live in London now it doesn't give you
the right to come back up here an' start tellin' us we're all peasants
y'know. We do know where London is. I mean it's only two and a half
hours away on the train. Christ you'd think you'd gone to the other end of
the world to hear you talk. It's ony a train ride away.
Peter (*laughing*) Not when you've only got a single ticket.
Linda Comin' up here, tellin' everyone what to do.
Peter I'm not tellin' you what to do?
Linda You think you can tell anyone what to do just 'cos you can get away
with wearin' women's boots . . .
Peter (*laughing*) You do what you like. I'm not tellin' you. Stay around here
if y' want to Linda. Have y' kids an' keep y' mates an' go dancin' an' go to
the pub an' go to the shops an' do all those things you used to tell me you
hated doing.

Linda goes to reply. Can't. Peter is waiting for her

Linda Get lost you! Well, I was young then. I mean y' do hate all those
things when y' young, don't y'?
Peter An' how old are y' now?
Linda Twenty-two.
Peter A twenty-two year old geriatric.

He looks at her. She at him

Linda You're a bastard y' know.

Peter I know. I'm a selfish shitty bastard because I did what I wanted to do.
I did the worst thing possible y' know, what I wanted to.

Linda An' why do y' think I should get out?

Peter Come on lovely; because you want to! Because while you're doin' all
this number you hate it. Y' do it, but while you're doin' it you hate it. You
want out of it.

Linda D' y' know somethin'? You are the most arrogant big-headed . . .

Peter I know. But I'm right aren't I?

Linda No. You're just so arrogant, you think you're . . . that you're right.

Peter smiles and shakes his head at her

Think what you like. It doesn't matter.

Peter (*after a pause*) Why don't y' jack it in up here? When we finish tonight
we're in the van and away—Scotland tomorrow, Newcastle on Sunday,
day off on Monday, on to Norwich, Southampton, couple of gigs in
Devon. Then back to London. Come with us.

Linda I gave you your answer a couple of years ago.

Peter But then I was askin' you to come with me. This time, lovely, I'm just
offerin' you a lift. You can get off wherever you want.

Linda I never accept lifts off strange men.

Peter Yeh. Well you should.

Linda Oh should I? God has spoken has he? Listen, Mr Knowall . . . it'd be
great wouldn't it, speedin' through Scotland with a second-rate band
when there's a hundred an' twenty guests stood in the church tomorrow
waitin' to see me get married.

Peter (*after a long pause; looking at her*) We are not a second-rate band.

Linda laughs. He puts his arm round her

Honestly?

Linda Yeh. Why d' y' think I came here tonight? It's the hen night.

Peter (*baulking*) Hen night! What? D' y' want us to play "Congratulations"
for y'? Or d' y' prefer "Get me to the Church"?

Linda Neither. Just give us a kiss.

*He does so. She looks at him, hugs him, breaks away, turns to the door of the
Ladies*

Thanks for lettin' me have me last fling with you.

Peter Hey.

She stops

D' y' love him?

Linda Accordin' to me mates I do. (*She opens the door*)

Peter Hey . . . do you?

Linda (*stopping*) What's it to you Peter?

Peter I'm tryin' to understand why you're stayin'.

Linda Look . . . don't you listen? I've told y', I'm gettin' married tomorrow.

Peter I wasn't askin' about that.

Linda (*smiling at him*) Tarar Peter. (*She enters the Ladies*)

He stares at the closed door for a moment before turning and going into the Gents. He heads for the urinal, sees Kav's drawing, stops to look at it. In the Ladies, Linda goes into the WC

The corridor doors fly open, Eddy leading the others

Robbie An' the weddin's off is it Eddy?
Eddy You're jokin' aren't y'? She might fuckin' say it's off. But no-one makes a laughin' stock of my mate.
Billy Too right. Yeh.
Eddy Thinks she's some sort of clever tart does she? We'll fuckin' sort her out. An' we'll sort out her fancy feller as well.
Robbie The fuckin' cheek of him—comin' up here an' nabbin' Dave's tart. He thinks he can just take whatever he wants, doesn't he?
Eddy He'll think again when we've finished with him. We wanna get him in here, right, away from the rest of his posin' mates. . . . Look Billy you go down the back an' see if y' can.

Peter having finished in the bog and taken another look at Kav's drawing opens the door of the Gents. He sees them

Peter All right lads?

Eddy blocks his exit, the others supporting him, crowding Peter back into the Gents

Eddy No sunshine, it's not all right is it?
Peter What?
Eddy In there. Go on.
Peter Look the——
Eddy In.

Peter backs into the Gents. They stand looking at him

Peter Well?
Eddy You what? You just shut it. (*He looks at him*) Are you a tart?

Peter looks back, sighs. Pause

'Ey, I asked you a question.
Peter No. I'm not a tart.
Eddy Well why have y' got tarts' boots on?
Peter (*after a pause*) I like them.
Eddy I don't!
Peter No. Well . . .
Eddy I don't like you either.
Peter Yeh. Yeh I'd gathered that.
Eddy Oh had y' now?
Peter Well . . .
Eddy (*after a pause; pointing*) You've been dancin' with our mate's tart.
Peter What?
Robbie While he's fuckin' lyin' sick in there.

Peter (*glancing at the WC*) Look, I didn't know she was anythin' to do
with——
Eddy You've been messin' around with Dave's future missis.
Peter Now hold on——
Eddy NO! You just hold on! Comin' back here. Posin' all over the place.
You can't just walk over us. Think y' someone special don't y'? Eh? You
think y' can fuckin' do things that we can't, don't y'? Well I'll fuckin'
show you what we can do . . .

*Peter backs away. Eddy grabs him, turns him and forces him to face Kav's
drawing*

That's what we can do! Look at it. Look.
Peter I'm lookin'.
Eddy Good.
Robbie That's fuckin' clever that is.
Peter I know . . .
Eddy Oh do y'?
Peter Who did it?
Kav Me.
Eddy (*to Kav*) Shut it.
Peter (*to Kav*) It's good.
Eddy We can do anythin'. (*He pushes him away*)
Peter Yeh. (*To Kav*) D' y' go to Art School?
Robbie (*laughing*) Art School! Listen t' the stupid get . . . (*He laughs*)
Eddy (*laughing*) 'Ey Kav . . . y' could be an artist you could! (*Laughing*)
Picasso Kavanagh . . .
Robbie Kav the artist . . . (*Camp*) Oogh can I hold y' brush for y' ducky?

Eddy and Billy laugh

Kav (*joining the laughter*) Art School! The only artist I wanna be is a piss
artist.

They laugh

Peter (*to Kav*) You stupid cunt!

Eddy wheels and grabs him

Eddy Don't you . . . don't you dare! I'm gonna tell you somethin' for your
own good—don't you come round here with your music, y' fuckin' music.
Don't you come makin' people unhappy! Understand? We'll be watchin'
you. You go near Dave's tart again an' your fuckin' number's up. Right?
Peter Yeh. Whatever you say.
Eddy She's our mate's tart. We look after our mates. We stick with them.
(*He leans in close*) You left this town. Y' walked out. You've got no claims
here. You left this town, so when you've finished tonight just fuck off out
of it! (*He pushes him away*) Get out!

Peter starts to go

Billy (*shouting*) An' don't come back. Y' big poufter.

Peter stops in the corridor and shakes his head. In the Ladies, Linda comes out of the WC and washes her hands

Eddy Right, come on. Let's find his tart.

They leave the Gents

 As they do so, the Roadie enters and sees Peter

Roadie It's no good Pete, the bleedin' place is——
Peter (*walking as if to the bandroom*) Good. Come on, let's get the gear packed and piss off.

Eddy and the others approach the corridor doors

 As they do, Bernadette and the girls come through

Bernadette We can't find her, Eddy . . .
Eddy We will. Come on.

 The fellers exit. The Lights fade in the Gents

The ladies continue on their way to the Ladies

Bernadette (*watching Eddy go*) Ogh . . . I wish y'd find me Eddy.
Carol D' y' fancy him Berni?
Bernadette I wouldn't say no to an hour with him. Come on.

They enter the Ladies

Linda What you doin' here? Why aren't y' out dancin'. There's not a lot of fellers left y' know Berni.
Bernadette You should be ashamed of yourself. (*Aside to Maureen*) Go an' tell Eddy she's here.
Linda Why should I Berni?

 Maureen goes into the corridor and exits

Carol Ignore your mates Linda. We don't matter to you, do we Linda?
Linda For God's sake, what y' on about now?
Bernadette Look Linda, you just listen to us for a minute.
Linda Tch . . . yes sir!
Carol See, see. Well don't listen Linda. Be selfish. You be a selfish bitch.
Linda (*after a pause*) All right. Go on. I'm listening . . .
Bernadette Listen to me Linda. Now I've been married quite a few years Linda. You're forgettin' that I've been through what's happening t' you. I understand.
Linda Well? Go on.
Bernadette Linda, there isn't one woman who doesn't have doubts the night before she gets married——
Linda Berni——
Bernadette Now don't interrupt me Linda! Every woman has doubts. But that's all they are, doubts. Y' don't act on feeling's like that. Just because you've got doubts it doesn't mean you can go rushin' into the arms of some ex-boyfriend an' then disappear with him——

Linda (*slightly warning*) Berni——
Bernadette What would happen if every woman did that eh? Who'd be married today if we all took notice of how we feel? Eh? Eh?
Linda Berni. Can I get a word in now?

She looks at them all. Their intensity is too much for her. She laughs

We see the fellers come through the corridor doors, led by Eddy

Robbie Eddy, don't be daft ... we can't go in there ...
Carol See ... see ...
Linda Look Carol ... look, all of y'. For your information I've got no intention of——

Eddy knocks the door open, points at Linda

Eddy Right you, out. Now!
Carol She won't listen Eddy. (*Glancing out to the corridor*) Hia Robbie.

Eddy and Linda stare at each other. Robbie and others hesitate outside the Ladies

Robbie Come on Eddy, we can't go in there ... It's the Ladies.
Eddy (*to Linda*) Get outside I said!
Carol I've told y' Eddy. She won't listen.

They stare at each other

Eddy All right, all right. Stay in here. I'll stay as well. (*To the others*) Get in here.

They can't

It doesn't bother me y'know. I don't care that it's the fuckin' Ladies—rules mean nothin' to me! (*To the others*) I said get in here!

Reluctantly they do so

Robbie Come on Eddy ... let's get out ... we can't stay in here ...
Kav Eddy, we're in the women's bogs ... come on ...
Eddy You stay where y' are. What does it matter where it is. Y' dont' worry about names on doors do y'? Names on doors don't bother me. I go where I wanna go. (*He turns to Linda*) Now you just listen to me. You might be Dave's tart, yes. But I'm his mate. I'm his best mate. He's our mate. You might try an' treat him like shite but we don't.

Linda glares

Carol Eddy's right y' know Linda ... you are makin' a terrible show of Dave.
Eddy Goin' round tellin' people y' not marryin' him—you! (*Pointing at her*) Don't you treat a man like that—understand? You just learn a bit of respect an' loyalty an' don't you go tellin' no-one that y' not marryin' Dave. 'Cos you are. Tomorrow!
Linda Piss off little man!

She quickly turns and goes into the WC, closing the door. Eddy, fast, bangs it open and grabs her

Eddy Don't . . . just fuckin' don't . . . you! Now you listen to what I'm sayin' girl. You play awkward friggers with me, you do it once more tonight an' I'll get that posin' bastard you've been dancin' with an' I'll break every finger he's got. Did you hear me, eh? We've already seen him. He's been warned. And so have you. Did you hear me?

Linda Yes. All right. Yes. OK . . .

He lets go of her but stays close

Eddy (*quietly*) He's crap y' know. (*He pauses*) He can't even play the guitar. (*He pauses*) Y' think he's good don't y'? Well he's not. (*He pauses*) I know about guitars. I play the guitar. Chords I play. G and F an' D minor.

Robbie Come on Eddy . . . if we're seen in here . . .

Eddy Y' don't wanna be impressed by him girl. He's all show. I could've been in a group. A famous group. I play the guitar. (*He backs out of the WC, turns to the other women*) She's all right now. She's come to her senses. Haven't y' eh?

Linda (*dumb*) Yeh.

Kav Come on Eddy . . . this is the Ladies.

Robbie Come on . . .

Eddy Right. (*To Linda*) See y' in church! Come on.

They go into the Gents

Come on. (*He begins running a bowl of water*) Get him over here, let's get him sorted out. I've had enough of this place. We're goin' the club.

They begin to try and sober Dave up by dousing his head in water

Carol Eddy was right wasn't he Linda?

Linda Yeh. Yeh.

Bernadette Oh Lind . . . Linda . . . thank goodness you've come to your senses.

Frances I'm always tellin' y' about your moods aren't I Lind?

Maureen comes through the corridor doors and heads for the Ladies

Bernadette Well I'm glad it's all been sorted out . . .

Carol Ah yeh. (*Arms around her*) Come on now Linda, eh? I didn't mean anythin' harsh that I might have said, Lind. All friends now eh?

Maureen rushes in

Maureen What's happenin'?

Bernadette It's all right Mo. Everything's fine now.

Maureen Ah I'm glad. Hia Lind.

Bernadette Now we can get back to havin' a good night, eh?

Maureen 'Ey, listen the group's not gonna be playin'.

Frances Why?

Maureen I dunno. They just announced it. There's not enough power or somethin', for their equipment.

Bernadette 'Ey, I bet I could put a bit of power in their equipment, eh?

The girls, apart from Linda, laugh

Eh Lind?

Linda (*smiling*) Yeh.

Frances What we gonna do now?

Carol Why don't we go somewhere else?

Frances What does Linda want to do?

Bernadette Linda only wanted to come here 'cos there was live music. If there isn't gonna be any she won't mind movin' on. Will y' Linda?

Carol Let's go to a club.

Maureen Ah shall we eh?

Bernadette Come on eh. Eh Lind?

Linda If you like.

Carol I'll go get the coats. Hurry up. We'll get a taxi before the pubs start emptyin'.

Carol goes into the corridor and exits

The others start preparing to go. In the Gents . . .

Kav Come on Dave . . . Dave . . . we're goin' down the club . . . have another bevvy . . .

Billy We'll have t' get in before eleven y' know. Yeh.

The ladies leave the loo. They approach the corridor doors

As they do so, Carol comes through with coats

They begin preparing themselves to leave. Linda leans on the wall, slightly apart from the rest of them

Eddy Sod it. Come on. Let's get him out. We'll get a taxi.

Frances I'll go see if there's any taxis passin' . . .

She goes through the doors

Bernadette (*to Linda*) All right love?

Linda Feel a bit sick.

Bernadette (*to the others*) That'll be all the drink. Don't worry love, you'll be OK tomorrow. Be all right on the big day.

The door to the Gents opens. The fellers come into the corridor, carrying Dave

Linda . . . close your eyes.

Linda does as ordered. Maureen crosses to her and turns her to face the wall

Maureen Turn this way Lind. Y' can't be too safe. God Linda . . . count y'self lucky y' cant see him. What a state.

Robbie (*as they approach*) All right girls.

Carol Hia Robbie.

Bernadette 'Ey . . . don't bring him here. We don't want tomorrow's bride seein' tomorrow's groom.

Kav He can't see anythin'.

Robbie He's blind.
Carol Hia Robbie . . .
Robbie Here . . . put him down here till we get a cab . . . he'll be all right.

They put him down, propping him against the wall. Robbie leaves the others to it and shoots across to Carol

'Ey, I was hopin' I might get a dance with y'.
Carol (*almost overcome*) Were y'?
Robbie Who's er . . . lookin' after y'?
Carol No-one.
Robbie No-one? Y' mean no-one's lookin' after a lovely young thing like you? (*He puts his arm around her*) We'll have t' do somethin' about that won't we?

Frances enters

Frances There's no taxis anywhere.
Eddy (*looking at Robbie*) I'll er, I'll go see if I can see one . . .
Bernadette Need a hand Eddy?
Eddy What? (*He looks at her*) Yeh. All right then.

Eddy and Bernadette exit

We see Maureen beaming at Billy who doesn't know where to put himself. Kav goes up to Robbie who is now necking with Carol

Kav Eh Robbie . . . y' were only jokin' weren't y'?
Robbie (*breaking*) What?
Kav Y' were only jokin' . . . about the clap? Weren't y'?
Robbie Yeh. (*Aside*) Sod off will y' . . .
Kav What?
Robbie (*breaking again; indicating Frances*) Go on.

Kav goes across to Frances

Frances There's no taxis.
Kav I know. It's terrible isn't it? Can't get one anywhere.
Frances Your name's Kav isn't it?
Kav Me real name's Tony. But they call me Kav.
Frances Oh.
Kav Hey.
Frances What?
Kav Come here.

She does

Frances What?
Kav Give us a kiss.
Frances Tch. Sod off.
Kav Come here. (*He gets a grip*) Come on.

He kisses her. She responds. Throughout the above, Maureen has been edging along the wall to Billy. She is now next to him. He tries to ignore it

Maureen Hia.
Billy (*not looking*) Hello. (*He coughs*)
Maureen I see everyone's made friends!
Billy Yeh.
Maureen Has anyone ever told you you've got "come to bed" eyes?
Billy I don't think so.
Maureen Well you have y' know.
Billy Have I? Yeh.
Maureen Tch . . . you're a real smooth-talker you, aren't y'?

She goes to walk away. He quickly grabs her and starts necking with her.
Linda turns and opens her eyes. Looks at the scene before her. Looks at Dave.
She crosses to him, bends down to him and quietly shakes him

Linda (*quietly*) Look at me . . . look at me . . . come on . . . just look once . . .
come on. (*She shakes him*) Look at me! . . . (*She shakes him roughly*) I said
look at me!
Carol Linda what y'——
Robbie Come here. (*He starts necking again*)
Carol But she's——
Robbie He can't see anythin' he's well away . . . come here . . .

They begin necking again

Linda Yes . . . that's it . . . that's it . . . (*She holds his brief gaze, drops him
back against the wall. She stands*)

Bernadette enters, linking arms with Eddy

Linda begins to walk down the corridor to the toilets

Bernadette You all right Linda?
Linda Yeh. I'm all right. Stay there. I'm just gonna be sick.
Bernadette (*to Eddy*) Wait here. (*She starts to go after Linda*)
Linda (*turning and pointing; vicious*) I said stay there!
Bernadette (*stopped by the force of it*) Linda!

She starts to approach . . . Linda backs away

I'm only coming to look after you love. You don't wanna be all on your
own when y' sick.
Linda Stay there . . . don't come near me . . . I'm warnin' y' . . .
Bernadette (*hurrying forward*) Now Linda don't start this . . .

*Linda goes to enter the Ladies. Instead, she looks across the corridor, rushes
into the Gents*

Linda! That's the Gents, Linda . . . Linda come out . . . y' can't go in the
Gents . . . She's gone into the Gents . . . (*To Eddy*) I can't go in there . . .
you go in, see if she's all right . . .
Eddy She'll be all right.
Bernadette Linda! (*She goes to the door, gingerly opens it and calls through*)
Linda . . .

Throughout the above we see Linda go into the Gents. She tries the large window. It is reinforced glass, no way out. We see her go into the WC. She comes out looking for something to break the window. She sees the towel dispenser and smashes it off the wall. She goes into the WC, closes the door and bolts it. There is a crash of glass. Linda exits

Bernadette goes in to the Gents. She tries the WC door

Eddy ... Eddy ... come here ...

He does so as she is trying to force the lock

Eddy, Eddy quick ... get that open.

Eddy puts his shoulder to it a few times. It flies open. Bernadette goes in

She's gone ... she's friggin' gone ... she's in that van ... quick Eddy, quick past the front ...

Cursing, Eddy rushes out into the corridor

(*As he goes*) Fuck ...

Eddy exits through the double doors

Bernadette looks out of the window

Y'won't do it Eddy ... y'won't ... she's gone ... you're too late Eddy ...
Kav (*prompted by Eddy rushing out*) 'Ey, come on ... Eddy must have got a taxi. (*He looks through the doors*) Come on there's a couple comin' ...
Carol Quick ... oogh quick come on ... someone stop them ... come on ...
Maureen Berni ... Berni ... come on ...

Bernadette slowly walks up the corridor

Carol Come on Berni we've got taxis ... we're goin' the club with the lads, come on ...
Bernadette Where's Eddy?
Carol He must be in the taxi ... come on ... get Linda ... come on ..

Carol exits with the others

Bernadette Carol, Carol hold on ...

Bernadette exits

Shouting from outside. It's garbled but as it dies away we hear Eddy

Eddy (*off*) Bastards ... come back ... bastards.

He enters, panting for breath

Bastards. (*He sees Dave, walks down to him, stands getting his breath back*) They've bailed out on us Dave. They've left us. (*Starting to pick him up*) They've all gone Dave. She's gone. She's fuckin' gone Dave. The bitch. (*He gets Dave standing*) Well fuck them all. (*He starts to carry Dave towards the doors*) They've gone. She's gone. Well y've got no baggage weighin' y' down. There's nothin' holdin' us back now Dave. We can go anywhere.

He carries him through the doors

BLACK-OUT

FURNITURE AND PROPERTY LIST

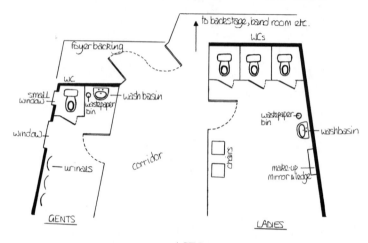

ACT I

On stage: **Ladies:**
    3 WCs
    Washbasin. *On it:* soap
    Paper-towel dispenser
    Waste-paper basket
    Chairs
    Long mirror
    Make-up ledge

    Gents:
    1 WC. *In it:* toilet paper
    3 urinals
    Washbasin. *On it:* soap
    Paper-towel dispenser
    Waste-paper basket
    Mirror on wall

Off stage: Pint of beer **(Peter)**
    Cable **(Roadie)**

Personal: **Girls:** handbags containing make-up, tissues, comb, cigarettes, lighter etc.
    Kav: pencil
    Eddy: quarter bottle of drink
    Peter: cigarettes and lighter

ACT II

Off stage: Pint of beer **(Peter)**
          Coats **(Carol)**

Personal: **Girls:** handbags as before
         Robbie: felt-tip pen
         Kav: pencil

LIGHTING PLOT

Property fittings required: lights in corridor, Ladies and Gents

Interior. Ladies' and Gents' toilets, a corridor. The same scene throughout

ACT I Evening

To open: Full general lighting in corridor, Ladies and Gents
NB Corridor lights remain on throughout

ACT II Evening

To open: Lights in Ladies, corridor
NB Corridor lights remain on throughout

Cue 13	**Robbie** and **Billy** enter Gents *Bring up lights in Gents*	(Page 35)
Cue 14	**Bernadette** enters Ladies *Cross-fade to Ladies*	(Page 36)
Cue 15	**Bernadette, Carol** and **Frances** exit *Fade lights in Ladies*	(Page 37)
Cue 16	**Peter** enters Gents *Bring up lights in Gents*	(Page 40)
Cue 17	**Peter** stops in corridor and shakes his head *Bring up lights in Ladies*	(Page 42)
Cue 18	The fellers exit *Fade lights in Gents*	(Page 42)
Cue 19	**Eddy:** "See y' in church! Come on." *Bring up lights in Gents*	(Page 44)
Cue 20	**Eddy** carries **Dave** through doors *Black-out*	(Page 49)

EFFECTS PLOT

ACT I

ACT II

See also Author's Note on page iv.

MADE AND PRINTED IN GREAT BRITAIN BY
LATIMER TREND & COMPANY LTD, PLYMOUTH
MADE IN ENGLAND